BRIDLE PATHS

TSCHIFFELY'S RIDE
From Southern Cross to Pole Star
CORICANCHA :
Garden of Gold
THIS WAY SOUTHWARD
THE TALE OF TWO HORSES

THE AUTHOR

BRIDLE PATHS

THE STORY OF A RIDE THROUGH RURAL ENGLAND

BY

A. F. TSCHIFFELY

THE TRAVEL BOOK CLUB
121, CHARING CROSS ROAD,
LONDON, W.C.2.

*This is an entirely new
Illustrated Edition
First printed January 1947*

*Made and Printed in Great Britain by C. Tinling & Co., Ltd.,
Liverpool, London, and Prescot.*

ILLUSTRATIONS

To
The memory of My Friend
"DON ROBERTO"
(R.B. Cunninghame Graham)
who
since I have written This Story
has set out on His Last Ride

CHAPTER ONE

Day-dreaming in London
Random Thoughts Lead to an Idea

THE END—the two short words I had been longing
to write. Now, at last, they were scribbled on
the last sheet of the messy manuscript before me.

Although a cigarette-end was still smouldering
in the ash-tray on my desk, my hand mechani-
cally reached for another " gasper," and before
I realised what I was doing I contemptuously
puffed smoke at the stack of paper before me.
Then, raising my head, I stared out of my window,
and vacantly observed the soot-covered brick
walls of the row of houses behind mine.

Below me, in what are supposed to be gardens,
were a few trees and square patches of lawn, the
colour of which almost matched that of the brick
walls opposite.

Not unlike Polar bears in their concrete rock
prison in a zoological garden a number of different
flowers were miraculously cultivated in this veritable pit of gloom, to the sight of which I had become

so accustomed that I even liked it—when I did not think beyond.

Dirty, impudent and noisy sparrows were holding parliament in a tree while two over-fed lap-dogs viciously barked and growled at one another through the rusty little gate which separated them.

Staring at the black walls opposite, I gradually began to dream, the magic wings of thought and recollection carrying me to far-away countries and regions I had seen—almost forgotten places which now seemed to belong to a dream, or to another life.

The brilliant sunshine of an exceptionally early summer brought back memories of the Argentine pampas, then I remembered Peruvian deserts, and long rides over the Mexican *meseta* with its golden sands, giant cactus plants, jagged *cordilleras* and snow-clad volcanoes in the far distance.

The faint rumble of traffic and the sight of the row of houses suggested a seething river thundering through a canyon. In quick succession panorama followed panorama; faces of people, adventures and amusing incidents, all whirled past my mind's eye like wind devils dancing over a sandy plain.

Pigeons flying past my window brought me back to reality with a start. Looking down at the papers before me, I again read the two words, " THE END."

Instead of the joy I had felt whilst writing them, they now made me feel sad and depressed, and my thoughts became so gloomy that I rose from my chair to walk up and down the study, feeling like a prisoner in his miserable cell.

Presently I stopped to look at a number of old photographs which adorn the walls of my study.

There was one of a prehistoric ruin in the heart of the Bolivian Andes, one of the rolling pampas, and another of the hot, shimmering deserts of Peru.

In the place of honour, above the mantelpiece, hung the pictures of the heads of my dear old equine pals, " Mancha " and " Gato," who seemed to be looking down at me with pity.

First I wondered what they might be doing while I stood there, gazing at them ; but soon the inevitable happened—for the thousandth time, memory and imagination took me back to the wilds.

Going afoot, hanging on to " Mancha's " tail, with faithful " Gato " following behind, the three of us slowly threaded our way up a steep Indian foot-trail in the rocky desolation of the Andes. Then, in rapid succession I remembered adventures and incidents I had completely forgotten since they had happened.

Suddenly my eyes fell on a set of bridles and a bit hanging on the wall. They were of the type used by the gauchos in the pampas, and had been presented to me by my friend, Cunninghame Graham.

Above the bridle hung another souvenir which I treasure more than I would the possession of a Koh-i-noor : a battered and greasy sombrero, which, in the now seemingly distant past, had often

9

done extra duty as water-bucket and nose-bag.

Suddenly an idea flashed through my head.

The manuscript—good or bad, whether it would be accepted or rejected by the publishers—was finished.

Why not see another bit of the world? Surely, to see beauty and life, and to find adventure, there is no need to travel far? Why not see England, meet its people, in villages, hamlets and farms, eat their food and drink their drinks?——

Although, off and on, I had travelled thousands of miles, through England, Scotland and Wales— by rail and by car—and in spite of the fact that nearly all my best friends in the world are of British nationality, I knew but very little about the country and the people who live outside of London—the gigantic whirlpool in which live many of my friends; friends in all stations of life, rich and poor, "respectable" and otherwise. (As the "respectable" will have it.)

Yes; London, the world's most amazing city, a stage of baffling and bewildering contrasts, the city where any type of humanity can be seen, where eccentricity and originality flourish, the Babylon where a relatively short walk takes one from the crudest street-markets to the luxurious and financially exclusive shops of Bond Street.

No, there was no need for me to study London, for even before the 1914–1918 war I knew almost every corner where life is to be seen, and since my return—three years ago—I had often wandered about, in the daytime, and sometimes throughout a night.

But how was I to set about it ? Sit in a train or in a car, and thus—without seeing anything—" do the country," as some American tourists say.

The thought of seaside resorts, with their over-crowded beaches, brassy promenade concerts and amusement parks, did not appeal to me.

When I imagined being in a typical English seaside hotel, with its little army of hustling waiters —whose facial expressions often remind me of performing dogs—its smell of food, and its pseudo-formal congregation of guests, a feeling of repulsion overcame me.

Of course, there would be a jazz band, dances, bridge (for the more conservative, whist) ; while the " exclusive " would sit in corners playing patience (pardon my ignorance, *solitaire*, I mean), or proudly read *The Times*, the *Morning Post*, or *Punch* (" *ça fait toujours une bonne impression* "). On rare occasions, some of the intelligentzia would assemble in small groups and talk about their wealthy relatives' estates in Scotland, or repeat imaginary conversations with members of the royal family, going on to discuss secrets of its intimate life, humour and " scandals," all of which are forgiven with smiles of supreme tolerance and understanding.

I had suffered such agonies before ; and I realise that such *raconteurs* only represent a tiny minority in England, although they are very much in evidence wherever the *élite* of stockbrokers, wholesale dealers, estate agents and similar worthies of society assemble.

During dances the younger generation of this breed of civilised people would discuss "art," which—as far as they are concerned—consists of cinematograph films and so-called "stars," glorified and made immortal in them, perhaps a few effeminate crooners, and leaders of jazz bands.

Then—horrors of horrors, untold sufferings of saints—I imagined a rainy Sunday in one of these hotels.

There was the lounge (with its infallible, anæmic palm-plants)—for all the world resembling a convalescent home, and I could see tobacco smoke, in the shape of haloes, almost piously ascending towards the ceiling. Only occasionally the rustling of a newspaper, a suppressed sneeze, or the sound of muffled coughing, interrupted a typical B.B.C. Sunday programme : orchestra rendering a seemingly interminable version of Fugues by Bach, arranged by A. Butcher, Mus. Bac., L.R.A.M., etc., followed by variations on the hymn, "We love the place, O God," and then perhaps, a lecture on Job by the Rev. Canon Goodboy, D.D., etc.

No. I had no desire to commit mental suicide. I had almost done this by the time "THE END" was written on the manuscript. For all I cared, carping critics would probably put on the black cap before pronouncing their verdict.

The coiled-up lasso hanging on my wall might

well have served as an omen ; but, instead, it gave
me an idea. Find a good horse, ride afar, in any
direction, just jog along, anyhow and anywhere,
canter, along quiet country lanes, over hills and
through dales—sunshine or rain—alone with a
horse to see the real England !

CHAPTER TWO

Horse-Hunting—Safety First—
A Peculiar Advertisement and Its Results

BROUGHT back to real life by expectant happiness, I immediately wrote to friends who are lucky owners of horses.

However, in due time I found that their animals were either unsuited for my purpose, some being too pampered, while others were too nervous, too big or too small.

One acquaintance very thoughtfully offered me a horse which, as the gauchos say, had all the *manias del diablo*. Among other playful tricks this heavenly pet had a habit of rearing up and of—sometimes—falling over backwards.

The kindly soul who offered him to me said that I surely would not mind this, and that I was the very man to teach his animal manners. " Two or three months with you," he added, " will just about do the trick ; and I shall be only too delighted if you will take him."

I did not doubt the sincerity of his last remark,

but I wondered what he meant by " will just about do the trick ? "——

Although, perhaps, my past does not suggest it, I am a firm believer in " Safety First." Accordingly, I insinuated that a transfer to another stable, or a journey to *Trapalanda** would be the best solution for the horse's future welfare—and mine, and proceeded to explain that English roads are harder than the soil of the prairies, and that forced landings on them, at speeds of over thirty miles per hour, and from heights from five feet upwards, are apt to be ticklish propositions.

Noticing that my listener eyed me with surprise, I added that if he doubted my statements and figures, the Ministry of Transport would surely corroborate or testify them to be correct.

The problem of finding a suitable horse was so difficult that, had it not been for the distance, I would have had my old " Mancha " brought over from the Argentine, for he would have enjoyed a leisurely jaunt through England, meeting its people, eating juicy grass and munching apples, carrots and other succulent titbits.

However, since this was out of the question, I finally decided to put an advertisement in one of the leading sporting magazines.

Accordingly I telephoned to a friend who happens to be one of the editors of such a journal.

When I told him what I wanted, he informed me that they were just " going to press," and very

* South American name for " horse-heaven."

15

obligingly offered to " squeeze in " my " advert," if I dictated it to him, there and then.

Having explained that I am not versed in the " telegraphic " art of wording advertisements, I asked him to be good enough to " knock " into shape, that I wanted a sound horse, in preference cob-type, to take me gipsying through England, Wales and Scotland, that I intended to make short and easy journeys, and that I promised good care and treatment of the animal.

This done, I thanked my friend at the other end of the line for his kindness, whereupon I happily went out to buy some good maps.

* * * * *

A few days later I was having tea with friends in a London drawing-room—between conversations thinking about gaucho parties in solitary *boliches* (inns) far out in the pampas—when, suddenly, I remembered my advertisement.

My hosts, who are regular subscribers to the sporting magazine in question, quickly produced the latest copy which had been delivered to them that day.

Of course, by this time they knew all about my plans, and were keen to see me succeed in my quest.

Their son, who happened to be at home on a school holiday, at once proceeded to look for my advertisement.

After having leafed over a few pages he found it, and began to read aloud :

" Wanted, a *pound* horse——"

" *Sound* horse," I interrupted, " *sound*, not *pound*. Please go on."

" *Pound* horse," repeated my young friend, " to take me *dixying* through England——"

" Don't they teach you how to read aloud correctly at Winchester ? " I said, snatching the magazine from the boy, and then I read for myself. Sure enough, he had read correctly, for there it was, black on white :

*Wanted, a pound horse—dixying—*and all about easy journeys and good treatment.

When I had read it all I tried to smile, but probably grinned as a man might if a friend stopped him in a busy street to tell him that he is wearing his trousers the wrong way round.

The other members of the party had a hearty laugh at my expense and—as can easily be imagined —this was followed by much good-humoured " leg-pulling."

Naturally, I did not expect that anybody would be likely to answer this advertisement, which suggested a practical joke.

However, two or three days later I was pleasantly surprised when, among other correspondence, I received several letters from people who offered me mounts.

* * * * *

Two enterprising owners of riding-schools had visions of earning easy money by recommending

17

their nags, stating that they were endowed with all the virtues horses had ever possessed.

One kind lady who had obviously read the book about my ride from Buenos Aires to New York, offered me the use of her pet. After many flattering, and quite unjustified remarks concerning my horsemanship, she had written several pages, telling me all about her animal, which must be unique in the world, possessing almost superhuman intelligence. In fact, by the time I came to the end of the letter I almost believed that this wonder-horse could do everything but play the piano, and that it would only drink Vichy water, and eat caviare on toast.

Having read another letter in which I was offered a pony, standing thirteen hands, but strong enough to carry a Polyphemus from Pole to Pole, my hopes of finding a mount had almost faded.

Finally, however, I opened a letter which gave me a ray of hope, and which was to lead to the solution of my problem.

A lady, writing from a country estate near Salisbury, offered me a mare, cob-type, of no particular breed, about fifteen hands, but very strong and sturdy.

The note was so sensibly written, and the enclosed photograph of the animal gave such a good idea about it, that I decided to make a journey down south to meet both the owner and the horse.

The letter, however, contained a passage which made me rock with laughter.

"I hope," the lady wrote, " you can bear it, but the mare is called ' Violet.' I did not name her ; she was given to me with this name. . . ."

Luckily my wife—whose name also happens to be Violet—saw the joke, and enjoyed it as much as I did.

To make a long story short, I visited Miss M.'s estate near Salisbury, and after I had been duly introduced to the mare " Violet," it was decided that I should return a few days later, and from her stable set out on my happy-go-lucky jaunt.

CHAPTER THREE

*Preparations for the Trek—Saddles, Bits and
" Hands "—Observations, Impressions and
Thoughts During a Taxi-Ride Through
London—Waterloo Station—A Strange
Coincidence*

BACK in London, I at once began to assemble the
necessary equipment for my riding holiday.

My friend, Cunninghame Graham, kindly
offered me an old-fashioned English saddle which,
in former years, had travelled hundreds of miles,
over the pampas and through the plains of Uruguay
and Venezuela.

For my purpose this saddle was ideal, any other
type being too heavy and cumbersome, and un-
comfortable for the animal. If I had used a
new one, most likely it would have produced sores,
for new saddles—like new boots—take time to
" break in," even if they fit perfectly.

Since I never bother much about the kind of bit I
use, I decided to take the one which was adorning
a wall in my study. It is of the type American

cowboys call " lady's leg," commonly used in the prairies and pampas, rather severe, and all the more cruel in appearance when used with rawhide bridles.

However, let it be remembered that there is no such thing as a severe and cruel bit. The hands behind it often make it so.

Personally, I ride with the reins loose, dangling down and swinging like the pendulum of a clock with every stride. Only when galloping I slightly gather them in.

Of course, I teach all my horses to be guided by the neck ; never by the mouth.

Even though riders of doubtful skill cannot make " neck-reined " horses look as smart and " proud " as they can when they have them fettered in all the contraptions Spanish Inquisitors ever invented, I prefer them thus ; for I like my animals to enjoy themselves while I am sitting astride on them.

Here let me make it clear that I am not referring to riding in polo matches, in show-rings, or in the hunting-field : refined pastimes which require " refined " methods, especially if horses have been badly handled when they were " green," and if their riders happen to be nervous " evergreens."

In order to get the maximum amount of pleasure out of a long distance jaunt, it is necessary to carry a minimum quantity of equipment. And it is surprising with how little a man (or a woman) can travel, especially in a country like England where one is never very far away from a shop or store.

As certain riders might wish to know what my equipment consisted of, a complete list and sketches will be found in an appendix at the end of this book.

At last everything was ready. My kit was assembled, business and the burden of private correspondence were put aside ; and, having plumped down in a taxi, I gave a sigh of relief.

As my " cab," a veritable old " liver-shaker," rattled along, the heavy traffic of London seemed to belong to another world.

Like a piece of drift-wood in a turbulent river, my taxi rounded Marble Arch and drove through a gate into Hyde Park.

When I looked at the cloudless sky and scorched grass I found it difficult to believe that I was in London, for although it was only ten o'clock, the sun was already so hot that it suggested a sub-tropical latitude.

The corner where Hyde Park orators expound their many theories—praising, condemning, glorifying, damning, piously singing hymns, or blaspheming in loud voices—was deserted.

Obviously, even those untiring world-reformers must sleep and have time to collect their thoughts and fresh energy for the next bout of verbal acrobatics.

As I rattled past this unique battlefield, I missed the sight of listeners around the different platforms with their banners, standards and inscriptions, and I regretted not seeing some of the orators I had often listened to when I had nothing better to do.

Of course, towards evening platforms would be placed there by the man who hires them out to anybody who happens to feel an urge to speak ; the price per hour, I believe, being one shilling.

Then the fun would begin : Conservatives, Nationalists, Communists, Free-thinkers, Protestants, Catholics, Nonconformists, Sinn Feiners, Church Armyists, Salvation Armyists, Pro-Armyists, Disarmamentists, Millenarians, Vegetarians, Anti-Sectarians, Semites, Anti-Semites, and an infinity of others, from mere blethering pups to composed octogenarians, would plead, implore, entreat, request, or urge their mostly passive and almost invariably good-humoured audiences to follow their ideals, creeds, theories, schemes and plans, and thus be led to their respective Utopian goals.

Coming out of the Park, near the beginning of Rotten Row where a few amblers were enjoying themselves, my taxi again entered into a regular whirlpool of traffic. While the driver slowly shunted towards the entrance to the Green Park, I looked—perhaps for the hundredth time—at the monuments which stand in the square in front of St. George's Hospital.

Almost opposite its main entrance I had a glimpse of a monstrosity in marble, representing a heavy howitzer—or whatever technical name has been given to these toys of modern civilisation.

Quite near this otherwise most appropriate and virile war memorial there is a very different example of monumental art : the statue of a Hermes. What a divine figure ! What elegance and grace of pose !

The ravishing young man's right hand caresses a heavenly hip, whilst his left limply rests on an inverted he-man's sword which might just as well be substituted by the magic wand of a fairy queen.

Oh, mannequins of Bond Street and rue de la Paix, you simply *must* see this divine figure, which would look perfectly gorgeous if dressed in the latest feminine creation.

At last my taxi cut out of the stream of traffic and merrily sped down Constitution Hill and past Buckingham Palace, with which, of course, I am intimately acquainted—from the outside.

Guards, in their picturesque uniforms, were stiffly strutting up and down outside the gates ; up and down—like automatons—along the narrow tracks which, during the course of years, countless heavy footsteps have gradually worn into the pavement.

Skirting St. James's Park I cut through Parliament Square with its stately old Abbey.

On my left I passed the buildings of Whitehall where Britain's silent but eminently efficient administrative work is done, whilst—ahead of me—

I approached the Houses of Parliament where, I understand, all the noise is made, and little work is done.

At the Embankment end of Westminster Bridge I caught a passing glimpse of the statue of Boadicea standing on her war-chariot—a worthy forerunner of the modern armoured car.

Drawn by a team of fiery horses, she appears to be racing towards the Houses of Parliament, as if determined to cut long speeches short with the terrible blades affixed to the centre of her chariot's wheels.

The Thames, with its barges, boats and tugs, always fascinates me.

As I looked along its banks towards Waterloo Bridge which, alas, would soon be no more, I could faintly see Cleopatra's Needle in the distance.

For the first time the word " needle " struck me as most inappropriate, for, somehow, I could not connect Cleopatra with needlework and contentedly purring cats.

If rumours handed down by historians are correct, this lady was not the prototype of a good Aryan *haus-frau* ; and yet, this " modern " " vamp " of ancient times knew so little about hypodermic needles that she used the fangs of snakes when she decided to take injections to make her forget all worldly vanities and sorrows.

At last my taxi pulled up at Waterloo Station where a porter took charge of my kit-bag which contained the saddle and the rest of my equipment.

When I had paid the taxi-driver he raised the little red tin flag of the meter, whereupon I heard the faint but melodious *cling* of a tiny bell.

The sound of similar bells has always been a source of amusement to me, for almost all ticket-punching contraptions in London seem to have a tiny bell inside.

On buses, in parks, at open-air concerts and in other public places where seats have to be paid for, people are given the privilege of hearing a miniature death-knell as they part with their pennies.

And to think that in spite of all this there are babblers who maintain that England's sons and daughters have no ear for music !

When I arrived on the platform, my porter indicated the seat he had reserved for me, where-upon, after I had given him a tip, he departed with a cheery " Thank you, sir."

Generally speaking, English people are the politest and most considerate I have met, educated or otherwise.

In few parts of the world would I entrust an unknown porter with my luggage, unless I followed close at his heels ; but in London I do not care where he goes, and what he does with it. I know that the man will do his job immediately and then wait for me, and that he will never try to extort an absurdly high tip.

In this respect I have had some very unpleasant experiences in other countries—in England never.

As usual, when I travel any distance by rail, I

bought several newspapers before boarding the train.

Later on, as I read to pass away time, I saw, under the title of " Famous Scoops with the Camera," a photograph of the sinking of the ill-fated *Vestris*.

The coincidence of seeing this picture in a train in England struck me as most extraordinary ; for six years before, after I had completed a ride of thousands of miles through the Americas, I had intended to sail from New York to Buenos Aires on the *Vestris*.

Fortunately, however, I was asked to deliver a lecture to the " National Geographic Society " in Washington, and therefore had to alter my plans, taking the next ship on which we carried thirty passengers who had been among the fortunate to be saved.

The photograph I am referring to, showed the *Vestris* listing terribly, whilst a row of passengers— one of whom happened to be a friend of mine— formed a chain by clasping each other's hands, in a desperate effort to lower a lifeboat.

It was strange that now, six years later, just as I was about to start out on another ride, I should be reminded of my lucky escape.

CHAPTER FOUR

*" New House "—A Fleet Street Sherlock Holmes
—Into the Heart of the New Forest—A Dios—
The New Forest, Past and Present*

AFTER a journey lasting about two hours I arrived
at Salisbury, where Miss M., the owner of the
mare " Violet," had kindly come to pick me up
in her car.

As soon as my kit-bag had been squeezed into
it, we started off towards my hostess's beautiful
estate, from where I was to set out after lunch.

Driving through a gate, an avenue of stately
old trees—half a mile in length—leads to " New
House," a beautiful mansion which, although the
name does not suggest it, was built in the year 1609.

Surrounded by beautiful gardens, inimitable
English lawns, ornamental hedges, clumps of
laurels, hollies, silver-firs, hoary old oaks and other
trees, and with an open meadow sloping down to a
pond with bulrushes—in and out of which swam
ducks and moorhens—" New House " ranks among
the most delightful old English homes I have seen.

28

When I thought that I was about to take Miss M.'s pet mare out of these lovely surroundings I felt like a baby-snatcher.

Before lunch I was shown parts of the house, objects of art and curios, among which I especially remember a most interesting collection of Nelson relics.

Just as we were finishing lunch, a servant announced that a press-photographer had arrived on a motor-cycle, and that he wished to see me.

As, accompanied by my hostess, I walked towards the ivy-covered stables, wondering how on earth a newspaper man could have discovered my whereabouts, I was amazed to see a friend of mine—who is a member of the editorial staff of a well-known newspaper—come trotting towards us, immaculately dressed in full riding kit, seated on an elegant hunter.

He had obviously noticed the surprise which must have been written on my face, for, after cheerful greetings, he explained that he had come down from London to see me depart.

When he explained how he had found out where I was trying to hide, and how he had obtained a horse to help him in tracking me down, I told him that he ought to give up newspaper work, and I advised him to apply for a job at Scotland Yard where the combined efforts of all the detectives could not have run me to earth quicker than he had done.

Just then the groom brought out " Violet," a

sturdy bay with a white blaze down her pretty face.

Standing about 14.2 hands, she looked like an inflated toy rubber horse, for since the hunting season had ended, she had done nothing but look after her bodily welfare—and obviously she had done it very well.

When I tried to put my saddle on her I found that the girth was about a foot too short, so Miss M. promptly offered me one which was almost long enough to fit an elephant.

The saddle and my small saddle-bags having been firmly fixed, I was ready to set out; but at the last moment my hostess decided to mount on a hunter in order to show me a short cut into the heart of the New Forest.

Whilst she was getting ready the press-photographer took a few snapshots, whereupon he departed, his motor-cycle sounding like the firing of a machine-gun.

The groom seemed genuinely sorry to lose his pet, and whilst we chatted, Violet looked at me with big, child-like eyes which clearly showed wonder and surprise.

Finally, after farewells had been exchanged, I mounted, whereupon, accompanied by Miss M. and my friend the newspaper detective, we set out. I could not help smiling to myself when I compared this departure with the one in Buenos Aires, when I had set out into the wilds of the three Americas, for on that occasion nobody took any notice of me—

nobody, excepting my two horses who did their best to get rid of me and the pack.

Led by the lady, my friend on his prancing hunter and I following behind her, trotting and cantering over narrow footpaths or tracks which were often completely hidden by bracken, heather or fragrant bog-myrtle. It did not take me long to realize that Violet was " forest-wise," for she never hesitated or slowed down (excepting when she snatched a mouthful of bracken or leaves off a tree), and where there were boggy patches or rabbit-holes, she either side-tracked, or jumped over them.

I was delighted to find that—like most New Forest ponies—she was neck-reined, for as already explained, I am not accustomed to—and do not like—guiding horses by their mouths.

Every now and again our approach scared rabbits who would hurry for safety, their fluffy white tails bobbing up and down as they fled into the thick bracken or into their holes.

Once or twice we put up a covey of partridges and other birds, and I caught glimpses of squirrels which, as if annoyed at our sudden intrusion, flicked their bushy tails up and down as they scampered up trees in rapid jerky movements.

Here and there sun-rays penetrated through the green roof above us, producing an effect which reminded me of light shining through stained glass windows of a cathedral.

Our guide had led us through this green paradise for about an hour, making us dodge overhanging branches and interfering twigs, when we came to a big clearing on a hill.

The three of us dismounted, and when girths and saddles had been tightened and readjusted, and final farewells had been said, my companions mounted to return to " New House."

For a while, as I jogged along, watching them cantering away, Violet tried to turn and follow them, but soon she settled down and went along quietly.

Occasionally she looked back at me as if wondering what all this might mean, and whenever we came to a path which led towards home she tried to go that way.

Soon I found myself in country I remembered fairly well, but during an absence of twenty years it had changed completely.

Rough roads, over which I had formerly ridden or driven in four-in-hands, had been " improved " to such an extent that they resembled speed-tracks over which a regular chain of cars whizzed as if fleeing from a catastrophe.

" Rufus Stone " (probably still encased in cast iron) was obviously still there, but on seeing a number of parked cars and a crowd of tourists who flocked towards the spot, I hesitated for a brief moment. Then, instead of visiting my favourite old spot, I turned the mare's nose away and went in search of quiet " drives."

Here and there, like ugly monster mushrooms, bungalows and houses had sprung up, or filling

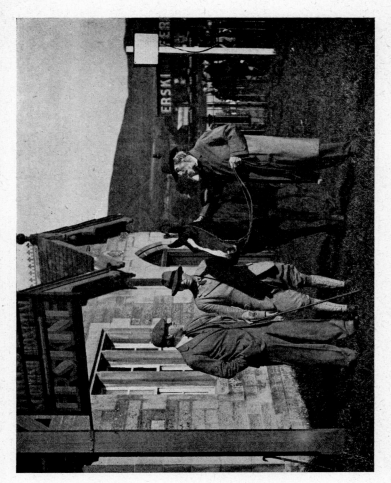

The Author and Cunninghame Graham

I set out on my happy-go-lucky jaunt

stations with their hideous advertisements, dis-figured what had once been corners of unsurpassed beauty.

Although I am still a relatively young man, I felt old when cars filled with over-painted platinum blondes, and dressed in beach pyjamas, tore past me, their young men friends joining in the screeching and yelping which reminded me of the parrot section in a zoological garden.

At last I found a quiet track where I could enjoy Nature at its best, while thinking about the past.

Towards evening I called at an old inn I remem-bered well : the " Trusty Servant," in a little hamlet called Minstead.

Years ago I had driven there with a team of horses ; but now, as I tied the mare to a rail on the little green, people watched me as if I had arrived with a unicorn.

After several knocks at the door, a woman appeared, and when I asked her if there was room for " man and beast," she looked at me with blank surprise, and when she had recovered speech, advised me that I had better go to Lyndhurst where I would have no difficulty in finding a stable.

Accordingly, I mounted once more and proceeded on my way.

I had gone some distance when, suddenly, Violet pricked up her ears and became very excited.

Listening with her, I heard a chorus of yelps and barks, and soon found that it came from the kennels of the New Forest foxhounds. The mare

33

obviously remembered the noise, for throughout the winter she had hunted with this pack. No wonder her excitement only abated when she had her nose in a manger filled with oats in a comfortable stable in Lyndhurst.

CHAPTER FIVE

*England's Public Friend No. 1—Lyndhurst
—The " Fox and Hounds "—Meeting Old
Friends—The Snake Catcher—The Parson
Blushes*

IN order to see England from a new angle, I had
made up my mind to avoid staying in hotels, but,
instead, to seek inns and country "pubs" where I
would be able to mix with people, talk with them,
and find out how they think and live.

Had I travelled in a car, many persons whom I
befriended during my ride would have given me
the " cold shoulder," and I would have missed seeing
and hearing many interesting and amusing things.

Even to-day the best passport in England is a
horse, for English people are probably the greatest
animal lovers in the world. In Britain the horse
very justly ranks as " Public Friend No. 1," dogs
taking second place by a short neck.

At Lyndhurst I stayed in a delightful old-fashioned
inn, the " Fox and Hounds."

Twenty years ago I had been teaching in a

private school by the name of " Park Hill," situated about two miles out of the village.

Although to-day the school no longer exists, I decided to stay in this neighbourhood for another day, for I longed to visit favourite old haunts and, for a few hours, to live old days over again.

After a good meal consisting of a large steak, fried onions and chips, I sat in the bar, conversing with the inn-keeper. At the old, beer-stained counter stood farmers and labourers who chatted over pints of beer whilst, in an adjoining room, bank clerks and nondescript members of the " better class " discussed cricket, tennis and sport in general.

Of course, they wore their old school ties or club blazers, the colours of some being glaring and sickly enough to turn African negroes white with envy.

Some of these heroes of the sporting and social world were accompanied by young ladies who, not to be outdone by their prototypes of the strong sex, wore "shorts," showing limbs which, I must confess, I repeatedly glanced at over my raised tankard.

Shove-ha'penny seemed to be the favourite game in the place, and I was fascinated by the skill some showed in playing this apparently easy and stupid, but, in fact, very difficult game.

During my conversation with the inn-keeper I heard about many people I had known in former years. Some were dead, but others were still " about and the same as ever."

Whilst we were talking, an old man, who wore a typical grizzled sailor beard, walked in and ordered a pint of ale, which the barman had already started to draw before the order was given.

Of course, this was " Hopper," the old ex-sailor who used to be the "handy-man" at the school. He looked exactly as he did twenty odd years ago.

Needless to say, he had more than his habitual daily pint that night, for talking about the past is apt to make old "salts" thirsty, even though they happen to be ninety years of age.

In spite of our prolonged session, I am glad to say that " Hopper "—who is now a gardener—has not broken the record of which he is rightly proud, for on the morrow he did not miss the first day's work in his long life.

Our stream of reminiscences and gossip was interrupted by a loud yet courteous, " Gentlemen, time, please ! " After glasses and tankards had been drained, and with sighs and grunts of content-ment deposited on the counter, the homely little crowd, together with a regular fog of tobacco-smoke, slowly drifted out of the door.

Standing outside in little groups, the infallible weather prophets' eyes were raised to the starry sky, and when the various topics of conversation had finally been exhausted, the speakers, after " good nights " and " see you to-morrows," slowly returned to their homes.

In the morning I awoke feeling slightly stiff. This did not surprise me, for I had done practically no riding for almost three years.

After breakfast I went to the stable where Violet

was busy stuffing herself with corn and hay, but, recognising me, she came to the door of her stall and looked at me, probably wondering if I had come to take her home.

If she thought so she must have been disappointed, for soon I made her trot over a vast, hilly, open space towards Park Hill.

I had heard that the old school coachman, George, still lived in his cottage, and I was looking forward to giving him a surprise.

He had always been a character, and I remembered that he used to earn a side-income by catching butterflies and moths which he sold to collectors.

To George the forest was an open book, and his knowledge of its denizens, their habits and haunts, from stags down to insects and snakes, was almost uncanny.

Often he had spent whole nights in the open, catching rare moths which he attracted with mysterious concoctions and tricks of his own invention, and, marvel of marvels, although he was a man of no education, he knew the Latin names of most insects as well as he knew the English pet names of the horses and ponies in his charge.

Just as I rode up to his quaint cottage, a man came out of its door. When I saw that he carried a butterfly-net and other paraphernalia necessary for bug-hunting, I knew that this must be George.

On making myself known, the expression on my old friend's face could not have shown more surprise if he had met a long-dead relative.

Once the ice was broken he said that he thought I was somewhere in the wilds of South America ; and then proceeded to tell me what had happened during my long absence.

With the closing down of the school the horses were sold, but in spite of the fact that the services of a coachman were not required by the new owner of the estate, George and his wife were allowed to stay in the cottage where they had been so happy for thirty years.

In order to live, the old coachman had then decided to take up one of the many strange professions the average man has never heard about.— George became a professional bug-hunter and snake-catcher.

He explained to me that grass-snakes, adders and other reptiles are always in demand to serve as food for certain birds and animals in zoological gardens, and that collectors paid good prices for rare butterflies, moths and other insects.

The New Forest has always been a place where extraordinary characters are to be met.

Among these used to be a dirty, ragged and unkempt man who, like George, was a snake-catcher.

An elderly gentleman who was a keen collector of snakes—an ophiologist, as he called himself— used to pay this snake-catcher good prices for specimens with rare or peculiar markings on their skins.

Now, as it happened, the bearded terror of New

Forest snakes had one great weakness, namely, a craving for alcohol. Invariably his hard-earned money went straight into the coffers of distillers and brewers—often highly respected and benevolent gentlemen who are indirectly responsible for not uncommon occurrences when people see snakes and other reptiles which in reality are not there.

However, there was nothing like that about our old snake-catcher, whose eyes never deceived him when he was out in the forest on business.

One day, as with his forked stick he poked about in a heap of leaves, his crafty eyes fell on a grass-snake which had most extraordinary white markings all along its wriggling body.

Before the unfortunate reptile had time to slither to safety, or even to hiss, it was safely inside the bag the man always carried for this purpose.

With a smile of anticipation the old snake-catcher followed tortuous paths through his green domain until he arrived at the house of the rich ophiologist, who surely would pay a good price for the unique specimen of snake in the bag.

A deal was immediately made, whereupon the old gentleman—who was an invalid—asked the great hunter to be kind enough to go to his study and place the singular snake into a jar filled with alcohol which he would find on the desk.

Thanking the buyer for his kindness, the snake-catcher went to do as he was requested.

Some time later, when the daughter of the house happened to go into the study, she was startled to see a bearded, dirty tramp stretched out on the divan, snoring melodiously.

Assisted by the strong arm of the gardener, the chauffeur carried the sleeper into a shed, from where, after having slept a sleep of the just, he made his way to his favourite " pub."

Although everybody in the house wondered what had made the snake-catcher so sleepy, the mystery was only solved when—some days later—the source of a most offensive smell was discovered.

Instead of alcohol, the jar which contained the coiled-up, and very much decomposed specimen of a strangely marked grass-snake, was found to be filled with plain water.

After a council of war the small assembly of amateur detectives came to the sound conclusion that the old snake-catcher had obviously thought that excellent pure alcohol would be wasted on a snake when his own body called and craved for it as a protection against the chills and dews of an early autumn in the forest.

* * * * *

Wandering over old haunts usually brings back happy memories, which are apt to be followed by a feeling of sadness.

This proved to be the case when I rode up to the gate at the back of the old school, which I hardly recognised owing to improvements and alterations its new occupier had made to the house and gardens.

41

The surrounding forest, however, was still as it had been in the old days. The same footpaths wound through the thicket and under giant trees which I remembered as if I had only gazed at them with admiration the day before.

Coming out into an open space I saw a number of forest ponies grazing among high bracken. Disturbed in their peace, they looked up, while a stag, followed by timid does, with graceful speed sought refuge in the forest.

Suddenly Violet began to snort and prance about as if in deadly fear ; and presently I noticed three donkeys behind a bush near us.

I then remembered having been told that the mare was afraid of nothing and that she never shied, except on seeing—a donkey.

She made such a fuss that I let her have her head, whereupon she galloped away as if we had been face to face with some dangerous beast of prey.

After a while she stopped and—from a safe distance—looked back at the three donkeys who watched us with typical, sleepy asinine interest.

Then, for some time, I amused myself by letting Violet do as she liked, allowing her to trot up and down, prop, snort and fuss until she grew tired of showing off.

As I continued my journey of exploration I wondered why donkeys were Violet's pet aversion and only fear, but after thinking it over, I came to the conclusion that this must be a lady's secret I would never solve.

Lyndhurst, the quiet old-fashioned village I liked to remember, had changed completely, excepting a few old landmarks which still remained.

Char-à-bancs and cars filled with tourists sped down the main street which had been " modernised," smelly garages and ugly filling stations had taken the place of homely stables, and the shop windows were filled with coloured advertisements depicting gorgeous girls (such as one never sees in the flesh) dressed in " next-to-nothings," eating chocolates, drinking orangeade, or smoking cigarettes.

As I was standing outside my inn, watching cars and people pass, my eyes fell on a figure which came wandering up the street, smiling to the left and bowing to the right, greeting people whose financial and social standing I could guess at fairly accurately by the various degrees of salutation of the benevolent looking man in black.

Obviously he was a local clergyman, for even if he had worn the clothes of an ordinary citizen, his face and mannerisms would have betrayed him as a spiritual shepherd walking among his flock.

I was wondering why parsons and priests insist on wearing such mournful uniforms which forcibly remind me of inquisitors or undertakers, when two girls in very *risqué* beach pyjamas passed the worthy gentleman who peeped over his rimless spectacles at a pair of shapely backs, liberally exposed down to their owner's waists.

Obviously the shocked parson decided that it would not do for him to be seen walking behind these girls, for he abruptly turned to the right to look into a shop-window where his eyes met the seducing glances of a cardboard figure of a bathing beauty who seemed to be inviting him to share a bottle of lemonade with her.

I could not help smiling to myself when the embarrassed gentleman turned quickly to cross the road towards me, perhaps thinking it was high time to deliver a strong sermon on the subject of girls so freely advertising whatever beauty God has been kind enough to bless them with.

CHAPTER SIX

Beautiful Hampshire—The Art of Path-Finding—Englishmen at Home and Abroad—The Unofficial Divorce Court Judge

NEXT day, avoiding the busy road as much as possible, I rode towards Romsey, one of the quaintest old places in lovely Hampshire.

At first I jogged in and out of the forest which became more and more open until, finally, I came to fields, every now and again passing homely farm-houses with their thatched roofs and modest though attractive flower-gardens.

The few men I stopped to talk to spoke with an accent which reminded me of the kind I had heard in the hills of West Virginia in America.

I have often wondered if the original settlers of that part of the New World were people who had emigrated from Hampshire.

It may interest readers to know that to this day some of these West Virginian " mountaineers," as they are called, still use old-fashioned muzzle-loaders to shoot stags and deer which abound in their wooded hills, situated within a stone's-throw of modern civilisation which has, as yet, left these fortunate people unaffected.

Some of the local terms used for the New Forest are—to put it mildly—odd.

For instance, tracks leading through the woods are called " Rides," more ornamental ones are known as " Drives," and similar trails, if covered with a down, grass, rough flint or chalk, are " Droves."

The last are really the remains of the old cattle droves which, in former times, ran over the down country and through the forest.

Then, also, according to the bewildering New Forest terminology, a grassy space in the open heather is a " Shade," and a clearing in the woods is a " Lawn."

I had arranged to spend the night with friends who own a beautiful estate near Timsbury.

When I arrived I was given such a reception that anybody might have thought I had just completed a transatlantic ride instead of a leisurely jaunt of a few miles.

The River Test, famed for the excellent fishing it provides for anglers, adds to the beauty of the surrounding country. Its clear, deep waters wave about masses of long, dark green weeds, in and out of which fish can be seen swimming.

Shortly after I had arrived at my friend's place, a gardener appeared, proudly holding a big pike he had caught.

Out of its formidable mouth stuck the tail of a

trout which was so big that the greedy cannibal had not been able to swallow all of it.

Violet had obviously done herself well in the adjoining farm where she fed while a party of us made merry until well after midnight.

My resolution to lead a simple life had been dashed on the rocks by my friends' hospitality. In the morning when I mounted to resume my wanderings, I wondered if the mare could feel the weight of my head, which appeared to be abnormally large and heavy.

As I gently trotted towards the unknown, I firmly made up my mind that in future I would never again overstep the border-line of moderation.

Whenever I conversed with farmers, the topic was usually about horses. Often I was taken to barns where I was shown the " old grey mare " who, of course, always was " the best that had ever been put into harness."

From farmers I sometimes heard about short cuts and bridle-tracks which enabled me to avoid riding over the hard roads.

Friendly advisers would tell me to go through a certain gate, maybe half a mile along the road, then keep on a path until it forked off to the right near an old oak tree, then keep on going straight until I came to another gate, and so on.

It can easily be imagined that—as often as not—I could not remember these indications, the result being that I finally found myself hopelessly shut in by fences, gates and hedges, or even lost, having to return to the place from where I had started.

Sometimes I found it even more muddling to return than it had been to come as far as I had, for, when facing in the opposite direction, the country-side often appears entirely different.

On such occasions I had even to follow the example of boy scouts, and do some track-reading, looking for fresh hoof-prints which never seemed to be there to my inexpert eye.

However, I was in no hurry, and never far away from houses or places where I could find something to eat ; and for the mare there was an abundance of grass wherever we went.

I made a point of asking farmers where I would be likely to find an inn with a stable, for I had no desire to arrive in a village late in the day, only to be told that there was no place where to put and feed the animal.

Thanks to inquiries I made, even before leaving inns where I had spent the night, I always obtained the information I required.

English country inns have a peculiar charm all their own. True, he who looks for modern comforts does well to keep away from them, but, to those who find comfort in good company, I strongly recommend them.

My usual lunch consisted of sandwiches, beer, cheese and bread, and, perhaps, a few pickled onions. Luckily, Violet—in spite of her name—did not worry about such trifles as a good honest onion breath.

Types of Hyde Park Orators

Statue of Hermes

Statue of Boadicea and "Big Ben"

On arriving at an inn where I intended to spend the night, I first of all made the mare comfortable. This done, I had a good wash which was followed by a frugal meal of whatever was " going " in the place. Later on I went into the tap-room where patrons discussed every conceivable subject, or made merry over glasses of beer, ale or cider.

Abroad, I have often heard it said that Englishmen take their pleasures sadly ; but if any of the people who think so had ever been in English " pubs " or inns, or at certain social parties and gatherings, they would soon change their opinion, for where could one find merrier crowds than at English country fairs or on English beaches in midsummer ?

When travelling abroad, or if in the company of people whose language he does not speak well, the average Englishman is self-conscious and shy, for he is essentially insular, besides being one of the world's worst linguists. Gauchos say about him that he is *bozal*, which means " hard " in the mouth, as are some horses.

Like their brothers all over the world, Englishmen prefer to drink in the company of other men, and I doubt that anywhere more liberality is shown than in an English " pub."

Individuals who otherwise are mean enough to take pennies off a dead man's eyes, insist on " treating " their drinking companions, even if the " round " represents the earnings of a day's hard work.

D

Admittedly this one-sided generosity is a two-edged sword, but since I do not intend to write a treatise on ethics or social reform, I will not go into details about the other side of this question, preferring to leave such matters to our wise philosophers, whose habit it is to repeat in their own words what others have said and written two thousand years ago.

Before it is possible to give birth to a new philosophy it would be necessary to invent a new Man—and I cannot imagine who is going to do this in order to improve on the interesting calamity which, like an undesirable drunkard in a " pub," was thrown out of the Garden of Eden.

In one inn, the name of which I do not mention for obvious reasons, I had an amusing though rather embarrassing experience.

The innkeeper who, soon after my arrival, had become very friendly with me, told stories about various foreign lands in which he had been stationed when a sergeant in the regular army.

At ten o'clock when the assembly of farmers was reminded that the establishment had to be closed, the innkeeper whispered to me :

" Sir, I can tell that you're a man o' the world. Don't go away, I want to 'ave a word wiv you."

Whilst watching the little crowd shuffle out through the door, I wondered why the man had whispered to me as if he had a secret of great importance to communicate.

As soon as the last tippler had reluctantly left the

place, my mysterious friend bolted the door, and then asked me to follow him into the back yard where it was as dark as in an abandoned coal-pit.

I was beginning to suspect all sort of things when my companion halted and whispered, " What I wants, sir, is your advice. I'm at logger'eads wi' the ole woman. I'm fed up wiv 'er, and you're the man to tell me what to do abaht it."

Having swallowed once or twice and nervously cleared my throat which, in spite of the pint of ale I had only just finished, suddenly seemed to be very dry, I tried to explain that this was a very difficult question I would prefer not to discuss with him.

In spite of my attempts to enter the house, the innkeeper kept me out in the yard, making me listen to his long tale of woe and matrimonial tribulations.

" She's bone-lazy an' a good-for-nuffin'," he said, summing up. " What I wants is a ruddy divorce, an' you're the man to tell me 'ow to set abaht it. I know," he added, " it's 'ard to get a —— divorce when there's been no scandal. But I'm sure you can tell me 'ow to fix it."

I began to wonder if my friend hoped I would offer to pose as co-respondent, or in some way help him to create a " scandal " which would help him to overcome the only obstacle he could see between the law and happiness, when a shrill female voice from the door announced that supper was ready.

" All right," my companion answered in a sulky, impatient voice, and then, to my great relief, led the way towards the house.

Whilst the two of us ate some uninteresting cold roast beef, pickles and boiled potatoes, I occasionally looked at the innkeeper's wife who sat in an armchair looking at the photographs in the *Daily Sketch*, every now and again raising her eyes to throw most unpleasant glances at her husband, whose food seemed to stick in his throat as if he were making efforts to swallow dry thistle flowers.

I had visions of retiring to bed in peace when, like a thunderbolt, the banging of a heavy fist on the table made knives, forks and plates jump and rattle, my host at the same time shouting, sending morsels of half-chewed food flying towards his startled wife.

" I've had enough of this, you ——. I'm goin' to get a —— divorce, an' this 'ere gentleman's goin' to 'elp me ! "

" Arrr, shurrup, you blitherin' idiot," said the wife, laying down the paper. " I've 'eard this so often that I'm gettin' sick of it. Eat your grub an' don't make a damned fool of yerself. I'm sure this gentleman knows 'ow to mind 'is own blinkin' business."

During the ensuing verbal combat I watched the two antagonists snarl at one another like two tigers. Every time I tried to worm my way out of the room, one or the other appealed to me for an opinion or support, which I cautiously refrained from giving.

At long last, when a semblance of temporary calm had set in, in order to get out of this unpleasant situation, I decided to fabricate a story which might make the two ex-lovers think.

With the convincing voice and mannerisms of an expert *raconteur* I told them about an acquaintance of mine who had once been in the same " fix " as they were now.

Going into all sorts of details about the unhappiness of my two imaginary friends, I went on telling my—by this time interested—listeners how the unhappy couple of my tale finally obtained a divorce which cost them over a thousand pounds, not to mention many other expenses and endless trouble.

The friend of my pathetic story finally was obliged to sell his " pub " in order to pay the weekly allowance of one pound to his wife, who was now so " hard up " that she could not even afford to go to the " pictures."

At last, unable to pay even one pound per week, my friend was locked up in the gloom of the debtor's prison where he was obliged to make mail bags instead of drawing beer for customers in his old " pub."

As I went on inventing sad details about the miserable existence of my two imaginary friends, I began to like my own story so much that I almost believed it to be true.

The innkeeper and his wife listened as two children might to the sad part of a fairy tale ; and when I finally summed up my yarn with the old moral, " Look before you leap," my host gave a meaning whistle, and slowly said, " Stroof, over a fousand quid ! Well, I'll be damned ! "

During the night I was awakened when the innkeeper—dressed only in his trousers and a shirt—entered my room with a weary cyclist who immediately curled up on the spare bed.

Before retiring, my friend, the would-be divorcé, came up to me and whispered, " It's O.K., the ole woman an' I 'as made it up."

Early in the morning, when I went to feed and water Violet, I found the innkeeper's wife, with a contented smile on her face, busy sweeping old litter out of the yard.

CHAPTER SEVEN

*Joys of a Leisurely Ride—Salisbury Plain—
Meeting Members of the " Old Brigade "—
The Influence of Hollywood—Marlborough—
It's a Long Way to Tipperary—Hints for
Would-be Dictators and Prospective Buyers of
" Pups "—Poaching—" Horsey " Lambourn*

RIDING along quiet roads and lanes I passed
through the delightful village, Mottisfont, with
its old church, surrounded by shady venerable
giants of green and pretty old cottages.

The weather was beautiful, and the temperature
almost tropical—which meant frequent halts at
streams or troughs to give the mare as many cool
drinks as she wanted.

Had I ridden at a fast pace this would have been
unwise, but since I never allowed the animal to
become overheated, good water could do no harm.

Whenever I stopped at a small store to buy cigarettes or a bottle of lemonade, Violet pushed her head
through the door, begging for lumps of sugar she
always received from kindly people who took a

delight in her pawing and neighing, begging for favours.

The Downs and Salisbury Plain, though in miniature, reminded me of places I am familiar with in South America.

From some of the hills I had magnificent views of the surrounding undulating country which is a sight never to be forgotten.

As far as the eye could reach, patches of cultivated land made the gentle slopes look like the familiar Dutch trousers, often worn on the stage and in fancy-dress balls.

Here and there farmers were busy harvesting their wheat and corn, their wagons, drawn by sturdy, well-cared-for horses, slowly moving along the symmetrical lines of ricks, as labourers skilfully loaded and stacked the golden sheaves on the vehicles.

The sudden change from sitting in my study to riding in the hot sun was bound to produce burns and blisters from which I slightly suffered by the time I reached Salisbury Plain.

My arms (I wore polo shirts with short sleeves) looked like smoked salmon, and short-sighted motorists might easily have mistaken my face for an over-ripe " Belisha beacon."

However, I soon reached the stage of peeling, and thereafter I was able to enjoy the brilliant sunshine, which accompanied me every day until I arrived at the Scottish border.

On reaching the outskirts of Salisbury Plain, I

hesitated for a while, unable to decide whether or not to visit Stonehenge, but when I had visions of masses of parked cars, char-à-bancs and flocks of modern Druids, I thought that Violet would sooner keep away from them.

In South America, especially in some jungles, I had to be very careful lest my horses ate poisonous grasses, herbs or leaves, but somehow I had never connected the English countryside with such treachery and danger, until, to my surprise, on reaching the outskirts of Salisbury Plain, I saw the following official warning, written on large boards :

HORSES — POISONOUS TREES AND PLANTS : YEW TREES, DEADLY NIGHT-SHADE AND OTHER POISONOUS PLANTS GROW IN THE WOODS ON SALISBURY PLAIN. GRAZING IN THE WOODS AND IN THEIR IMMEDIATE VICINITY IS PROHIBITED.

Avoiding woods I trotted and cantered over the Plain, thankful to the authorities who are responsible for these written warnings.

Leaving Salisbury Plain behind me, I rode towards Marlborough, passing through quaint old Wiltshire villages and picturesque hamlets.

Taking it easy I had ample time and opportunities to admire many old farms and houses with their thatched roofs and homely diamond-paned windows. The neat little gardens and geraniums in front of windows spoke well of the people who inhabit these homes which, in many cases, had been built generations ago by forefathers of the present-day occupiers.

In some villages I passed through, old men sat on benches outside their favourite inn, or, perhaps, on a circular bench built around the base of a huge old tree at the cross-roads in the centre of the place.

As I approached them to give the mare a short rest in the shade, these veterans would watch me with critical eyes, their bearded chins resting on the handles of walking-sticks.

I had many long conversations with such local patriarchs, who were delighted once more to see a man travel on horseback.

During our friendly chats, chiefly about horses and the " good old days," I usually asked for information about bridle-tracks or lanes in the neighbourhood, or tried to find out where a good inn with stabling accommodation could be found.

Every time a car filled with tourists sped past us, the old men would growl and murmur curses, and more than once I was told, " Dammit, if I wasn't old I'd git an 'orse an' join ye, for that's the way to see the country, not in one o' them crazy machines. —Awrrr ! "

The young generation in such villages offers a strange contrast, especially the girls, who—like many of their sex in cities—foolishly, and often ridiculously imitate some film star of their dreams, especially in the manner of wearing their hair.

If the fact that most of the modern English girls take more pride in their appearance than did their sisters twenty years ago, can with any degree of justification be attributed to the influence of the cinematograph, this would be about the only thing to be said in favour of this new system of exploiting and even corrupting the masses who will do and pay anything to avoid the fatigue of thinking.

Since in all villages of any size, going to the " pictures " is the chief form of entertainment (chiefly among the young), it is not surprising— many films shown being of Hollywood origin— that American slang is widely used, even by children.

I vividly remember admiring an old Tudor house, in front of which children happened to be playing. Two little boys suddenly began to quarrel, whereupon one of them shouted to the other, affecting a strong nasal twang which would have done any Bostonian honour : " Scram, you lousy guy, scram ! "

Not to be out-done in this verbal duel, the other boy, screwing his mouth to one side, snarled with the best Bronx intonation : " Oh, yeah ? "

Coming out of the beautiful Savernake Forest through which I had vainly tried to follow a track I had been told about, I saw Marlborough in a valley below me.

On entering the town I asked a policeman if he knew of a stable where I could put the mare.

Guided by his information I proceeded, and

presently halted at the door of what looked like a fairly good hotel.

A tall commissionaire, dressed in a " gaudy " uniform, his chest bedecked with enough medals to make even a Hermann Goering thin with envy, slowly strode from the door to ask me what I wanted.

The man cast such haughty glances at me that I felt like a recruit facing his commanding general for the first time.

Judging by the twitching points of the commissionaire's waxed moustache he had his doubts about my integrity or respectability, but after a few more searching glances announced that he would consult with his superiors.

By this time a small crowd of curious spectators had assembled, probably wondering if I was the advance guard of a travelling circus.

Presently the commissionaire reappeared, gently but with authority pushing aside bystanders in order to pass.

When he pompously—though politely—inquired how long I intended to stay in the hotel, I told him not to bother any more, for while he had been inside consulting with the " superior staff," one of the spectators had told me about excellent stables which were situated only about a quarter of a mile from where I stood.

As soon as the mare had been made comfortable I went to an inn where I found everything I needed.

After having eaten a hearty meal I strolled about the town to see the sights.

In the main square, a market was in full swing, travelling vendors shouting in loud voices, trying to convince hesitating buyers that their oilcloths, carpets, rugs or shawls, though only half a crown per ten yards, were of better quality than the most expensive sold in the " swankiest " London stores.

Wandering about, I came to the portals of Marlborough College, one of England's leading public schools.

Although, in many ways, I am an admirer of these institutions, I have never been able to understand why they are called " public," unless the word means " well-to-do."

A territorial force had an encampment on a hill overlooking the town. As the men were to be dismissed on the following day, saloons and " pubs " were filled with merry crowds of sunburnt and bronzed men in uniform.

In the tap-room of my inn, vocal cords were being strained, singing, cracking jokes and laughing, until, after some time, a pompous sergeant managed to get the floor to himself, telling his listeners all about the " behind the scenes " of the test matches against the " Aussies," whom he slandered and bespattered in language which did full honour to one of his rank.

I was sorry when, in the name of " DORA," the merry crowd had to be almost pushed out of the place to finish good stories and important discussions out in the street.

Even when I was in bed I heard sudden bursts of

laughter below my window, and lusty, though rather " beery," voices singing songs as warriors slowly returned to their camp which was to be no more next day.

The subject being *SOLDIERS* brings to my mind an observation I have often had occasion to make.

The average Englishman—in the Prussian sense of the word—is not a born soldier, for, unless the occasion arises, he shuns the wearing of a uniform, and avoids fighting.

I have witnessed several smart Sunday parades, at the conclusion of which the officers—from the general down—rushed to put on civilian clothes.

This does not mean that they are not proud of their uniforms, for I can imagine no more martial a bearing than that of British soldiers on ceremonial occasions.

Englishmen hate what the French call *chi-chi*. Arrogant and bellowing sword-rattlers of the be-medalled and be-plumed modern dictator type would not even draw a crowd in Hyde Park. In Petticoat Lane, perhaps, if they demonstrated with patent chest expanders, sold ice-cream, " tips " for the races, medicines, or hair-restoring concoctions.

Anybody who does not know Petticoat Lane (not far from Liverpool Street station) ought to visit it at the first opportunity. Every Thursday and Sunday a unique market is held there.

On Thursdays this market is chiefly patronised

by Jews, but on Sundays the Children of Israel cater for the Christian " mugs " who swarm there to buy anything from antiques down to contraceptives, whilst, not far away, you can imagine bishops, deans and canons preaching about lofty principles of life and Resurrection Day.

Although I am breaking up my story, I must mention another most interesting Sunday market in the East End of London, not far from Petticoat Lane.

If anybody wishes to buy a "pup" (perhaps in both senses of the word), a canary, or any living animal with or without hair or feathers, there is another market in Club Row.

However, if a person buys a pet there, he or she must be prepared to see great changes after it has its first bath, for maybe, an " Irish terrier " will turn out to be a multi-coloured, one-volume edition of canine breeds ; or a canary's bright plumage may change from lovely picric yellow to brown, until, finally it will be recognised as a common sparrow.

Years ago I bought a " pup " in Club Row, so I can speak from personal experience.

* * * * *

When I left Marlborough it was my intention to make a long journey through the beautiful country between there and the Berkshire downs, but when I stopped to have lunch at an inn in Ramsbury, I met a merry assembly of farmers who soon became so friendly that they would not let me go.

Before I had time even to put in a mild protest, the mare was taken to a nearby farm which belonged to two brothers who formerly had been sheep-breeders in the Argentine.

Never have I seen a more homely and amusing assembly of local characters than I found in this tap-room in Ramsbury.

In the afternoon some of my new friends made me walk miles to see the surrounding country, all the while teasing each other with good-humoured back-chat.

Two or three of my guides seemed to have a rare eye for detecting fresh rabbit or hare runs, and even the most timid pheasant sneaking to a hiding-place did not escape their eagle eyes.

By degrees the conversation veered to technical details connected with the art of poaching. As I listened I came to the conclusion that my education was sadly lacking, and I felt as a young missionary might on hearing head-hunters discuss their various tricks for trapping human victims.

Following my trusty guides through beautiful woods and dales and over hills, I gradually began to take such an interest in their conversation that I wished it were dark, for, like a bottle-fed tiger-cub on smelling meat for the first time, a hitherto dormant instinct had been awakened within me.

A few days later, in a place I will not mention, I had the thrill of acting as assistant to poachers, spending a whole night crawling, or squatting behind hedges. Being a novice, I was only allowed to carry a bag, which was quite heavy by the time the first rays of purple in the sky gave us the warning to return to the farm. The only possible clue we left behind in a hollow was an empty whisky bottle I had taken with me (full, of course) as an initiation fee into one of the oldest crafts.

My fellow criminals told me many amusing yarns connected with poaching, and amazed me with a demonstration of the marvellous way in which they train their dogs. The exhibition I saw was fit to be presented before kings and princes, who would probably enjoy it more than the weighing of babies in maternity hospitals, football matches between rival teams of centenarians, and similar penalties of their exalted rank.

Gentle reader, you may hate and despise poachers, and disapprove of me for having mixed with such people, but I assure you, some of these men are fine " sports "—and great artists.

From Ramsbury I had a most enjoyable ride, reaching the Berkshire Downs by following a grass-covered track, friends had told me about.

Unfortunately, I must have gone the wrong way at some point, for, instead of avoiding villages, I suddenly found myself in Lambourn, a place famous for its racing-stables.

Even if I had not known about these, I would soon have guessed that this must be a " horsey " place, for almost every other man I saw there had the

E

word *HORSE* written all over him, as is often the case with grooms, horse-dealers, or people who, owing to constant association with our four-footed friends, have acquired equine minds.

Diminutive, ape-like creatures, known as jockeys and racing-stable grooms, with their thin, bandy legs encased in leggings, waddled about like alligators on *terra firma*, the flat feet of some bringing to mind waddling ducks.

Yes, Lambourn certainly has an atmosphere.

Riding out of the place I came to a steep incline which leads up a hill. At the top, having reached a flat stretch covered with a down of soft turf, I decided that this was an ideal place for a canter.

Going merrily along, I noticed lines of posts and chains, the purpose of which never dawned on me until my canter came to an end near a small wood.

I had been much too busy looking at the delightful scenery around me to realise that my mare had been trespassing on sacred ground where the aristocracy of the English turf is trained. She had cantered over the " gallops " of Lambourn—an offence as unheard-of as riding up the aisle of a venerable cathedral.

CHAPTER EIGHT

*The Berkshire Downs—Memories and Meditations
of a Globe-Trotter—Oxfordshire—Perils of Modern
Roads—An Old Cart-Man Talks—Adventures in
Old Oxford*

ON reaching the top of a hill I dismounted to
let Violet graze whilst I admired the surrounding
country which, from where I sat, suggested a vast
continent.

As far as the eye could reach I saw hills, gentle,
undulating slopes and plains, the wooded patches
and cultivated fields on them forming designs like
futuristic jigsaw puzzles.

To give life to this delicately-coloured picture of
a strange fairyland, shadows of snow-white clouds
chased each other, momentarily changing the tints
of the patterns on the countryside below.

The hedges, intersecting lanes and fences formed
strange designs which reminded me of my first
impression when I looked at a geometry book in
the days of my childhood.

As soon as the drifting shadows had passed over
certain slopes and fields, the colours appeared to

be even brighter than they had been before, gold, green, purple and many other colours and shades vibrating as if greeting the reappearance of the sun.

The snorts of contentment between the regular noise of munching came from Violet who grazed near me. This, together with the rustling of the grass with which a soft breeze played, causing it to move like waves, made me delightfully dreamy.

Soon, like the shadows chasing each other over the distant hills, memory began to follow memory.

Now I was in the immensity of the pampas, then in the desolate vastness of the Andes, and even in the green wilderness of some Central American jungle. I remembered their majestic, overpowering beauty, which inspires a feeling of fear and utter futility, for such regions, like the sea, pass human understanding. True, some men are wont to dabble in them, some bold ones even pretending to understand their mysteries.

No wonder that men who spend their lives in the imposing solitude and vastness of such places are fatalists, for they realise the futility of Man. The grandeur and immensity of their surroundings constantly reminds them that they are mere nothings, but yet, being human, they try to deceive themselves into believing they are immortal.

I was still day-dreaming when the cigarette burnt my fingers, the sharp pain bringing me back to reality.

Hissing something to myself, I tossed away the cigarette-end, in doing so making Violet glance at me with wondering eyes, but without interrupting her grazing. . . .

In spite of our rapidly spreading civilisation, with its concrete speed-ways, petrol fumes, mass produced bungalows and advertising posters (to mention only a few of its harmless manifestations), England can be proud of possessing many beauty spots which are, as yet, unspoilt.

Let poets write about balmy tropical breezes, waving palms, silvery moons and myriads of bright twinkling stars reflected on tropical seas with their phosphorescent flashes, in their fits and spasms of "inspiration," or owing to total ignorance of facts, omitting to glorify mosquitoes, gnats, sand-flies, suffocating heat, poisonous plants, fever and disease. Let them forge words and juggle with them, but give me the cool breezes and clear streams of temperate zones, fields of green and gold ; the only paradises fit for gods, and the men who made them.

I could have sat for hours, dreaming and gazing at the scenery surrounding the Berkshire downs, but I had to move on. Surely I would come to other delightful spots on my journey.

A bridle-track led down the hills towards Wantage, from where I turned my mare's nose in a south-easterly direction, to ride through quiet country lanes towards South Moreton, a little place near Wallingford, where my friend Peter Belloc and his family gave me a hearty welcome in their home.

I felt sorry for my host when, next morning, he had to leave for his office in London, while I saddled up to wander wherever fancy would lead me.

As it happened I chose a route which, though picturesque and interesting, is not fit to ride over on horseback. Try as I would I could find none other but asphalt roads which led towards Oxford.

Farmers were busy harvesting wheat, some feeding modern threshing machines in the fields while others slowly drove huge loads towards their farms. For some time I rode alongside a wagon, conversing with an old carter who was driving it.

Being one of the "old brigade," he naturally hated the cars which incessantly raced past us, some of their drivers slowing down to curse him for allowing his horse to walk in the middle of the road where the animal was less likely to slip.

Being built in *fish-back* shape, modern motor-roads are totally unfit for horse-drawn traffic. In keeping to one side, the unfortunate animals have to walk on a considerable slope, which makes the pulling of heavy loads most difficult, to say the least.

For riders, sidings are supposed to be provided, but where such exist they are intersected by little trenches or channels for draining water from the road. Often these channels are dangerous, especially when they are made invisible by grass.

To add to the annoyance, and even danger, heaps of gravel, crushed stones and sand obstruct the sidings, obliging riders to go out on the slippery road where many passing motorists have little or no consideration for horses, apparently not realising that, in the event of an accident, they are as much in peril as are the horses and their riders.

As we went along, side by side, my friend the carter emptied his heart to me, but after we had halted at a wayside inn *to give the horses a rest*, the balm of a pint of ale made the old man see the bright side of life.

After that, until we parted company at a cross-road, he told me stories about " 'orses " he had handled in his time, talking about them with an affection that was almost touching at times.

Pointing at the sluggish equine veteran in the shafts before him, he proudly told me that—not long ago—on seeing an elephant in a village street, the horse had bolted like a streak of lightning— wagon and all—running like a Derby winner until he finally stopped at the door of his stall.

Even though some of the old man's stories were, perhaps, not strictly true, I went over them again in my mind until, going down a steep hill, I saw colossal gasometers in the distance. Behind them, I knew, lay hidden Oxford, the famous seat of learning, the spiritual home of oarsmen who would like to see light-blue turn black.

Having passed through the outskirts of the town, consisting chiefly of modern " bungalow-villas," filling stations, small stores and concrete roads, I approached the centre of old Oxford.

From MY *seat of learning* I admired venerable buildings while people, surprised at the apparition of a sunburnt man with such unconventional riding equipment as mine, stared as if I had come from the planet Mars.

Guided by the directions a policeman had given me I slowly approached the very centre of the town, where traffic is controlled by red, yellow and green lights.

I had been told that on the other side of the main whirlpool of buses and cars I would find a stable in a side street.

The mare took not the slightest notice of even the biggest and noisiest vehicles, but when a green light gave us the signal to pass through the small, congested square where several streets meet, she suddenly began to fuss—a thing she had never done before.

Spinning round, dancing sideways, propping, going backwards and doing everything but stand on her head to whistle " Abide with me," she went through her repertoire of tricks, holding up all the traffic.

Perhaps she had suddenly realised that she was in Oxford, or, being susceptible to psychic influences, an atmosphere impregnated and saturated with profound human wisdom had affected her.

A few minutes before her undignified and unlady-like display, I had visions of leaving Oxford with my nasal passages duly attended to by a local specialist, thanks to whose skill I hoped to be able to speak the English language as it is spoken by some of the intellectual graduates.

However, before an officer of the law—who had come to assist me in my dilemma—had finished his lecture, I came to the conclusion that my elementary vocabulary of pure English was still lamentably poor, so I decided first to lay the necessary foundations before passing on to the giddy heights of grammar, diction and the refined accent befitting a super-Oxonian scholar.

With the sound of plain English and the echoes of motor-horns, sirens and bells still in my ears, I reached a stable-yard where I dismounted like a wet towel slipping off the edge of a bath-tub. . . . The first lecture was behind me.

Later, when I had summoned fresh courage, I meekly wandered around the town, admiring some of its places of interest. Feeling really bold, like a daring fox sneaking into a chicken-run in broad daylight, I even slid through the ancient portals of a college.

Instead of poultry, I ran into a flock of cackling American tourists who, guide-books in their hands, stared at a monument, wondering who the *cute guy* in bronze might be.

Realising that the university was in recess, I hurried back to the stables where, seated on a bale of hay, I read Cobbett's *Rural Rides* while horses in their stalls snorted in a language I could understand.

What with the university temporarily closed, and the only academic conversation in public bars being the latest news about the test matches with Australia, Larwood, Voce, M.C.C. and a mysterious " leg-theory," " body-line bowling " and other mysteries of a very exact though much disputed science, I came to the conclusion that Oxford is no place for me, so I decided to return to earth early next morning.

CHAPTER NINE

Farmer and Huntsman—Base-Ball—Broadway
Melody—The Pronunciation of English Names
— Evesham— Carnival— Stratford-on-Avon—
Shakespeare, Mae West and " Gentlemen "—
Warwick Castle

NOT far out of Oxford I found some ideal lanes
which I followed in the direction of Chipping
Norton.

During the afternoon the sky suddenly darkened,
and soon a heavy shower began to fall, obliging
me to seek shelter under a spreading tree.

Presently a farmer, who was busy ploughing a
field, joined me. Like most English farmers, he
proved to be a great sport, and very fond of
hunting.

In the course of our conversation he told me a
great deal about what hunting used to be, and what
it is to-day, making some very caustic remarks
about modern young huntsmen who hire horses for
the day, to race the " guts " out of them, damage
fences and leave gates open.

75

After about twenty minutes the sky began to clear, and soon after the sun shone again, as it continued to do every day until I had crossed the Scottish border.

In Chipping Norton I found a stable and comfortable quarters, and spent the evening in the tap-room where I joined in conversations, at the same time watching experts play " darts "—a simple enough game at first sight, but an art which requires long practice (and many pints of ale) before a man can hope to qualify for the honours that go with a local championship.

That evening there was great excitement in the tap - room where everybody discussed a " ball-game " which had been played during the afternoon.

As " ball-game " sounded rather American to me, I inquired what branch of sport they were talking about, whereupon, to my surprise, I was told that it was base-ball.

Enthusiastic " fans " said with pride that this game was played in Chipping Norton long before it became popular in America. In fact, some of the men in the bar assured me that the game of base-ball originated in their village.

This statement, for all I know, may be perfectly correct, and I leave it to students of the history of this game to decide as to whether or not the enthusiasts in Chipping Norton were right in their assertion.

There being good grass skirtings along the main

road to Evesham, I took this route which led through picturesque country and old-fashioned hamlets.

Many of the houses in this neighbourhood are built of stone, and the roofs are tiled with what appears to be grey slate.

Out of cracks and spaces in the walls grow ferns, lichen and even flowers, blending to perfection with patches of moss and the colour of the weather-stained stones which are peeling and chipping with age.

Reaching the top of a hill, I beheld a wonderful panorama of the Malvern and Welsh hills in the hazy distance, looking like gigantic dark purple billows at the horizon of a rolling sea of green.

A winding road led down to Broadway, a very much modernised " olde " village which, perhaps, owing to its name, attracts flocks of American tourists.

In this neighbourhood Mr. Henry Ford bought an old forge which he had " transplanted " to America where it must look as an Indian wigwam would in Piccadilly Circus.

Although most of Broadway's " ye olde " shops are of modern vintage, the place has sufficient synthetic " Old England " atmosphere to attract char-à-bancs packed with modern " Mayflower " pilgrims who stalk and nose about, " shootin' " *cute* corners and cottages with their Kodaks.

Near Broadway, nestled against a hill, lies a little hamlet called Snowshill.

Should a traveller ask a local farmer what the place is called, the answer would be " *Snozzle*," for no patriotic inhabitant of Snowshill wishes the name of his native hamlet to be connected with the words *snow* and *hill*.

When I consider how names, such as Beaulieu, Cholmondeley, Beauchamp, St. Mary's Cray, Marjoribanks, and many others are pronounced, I think that in my case it would be quite justifiable if, for the sake of convenience and democracy, I pronounced the complicated collection of consonants of my name as, *Smiffy*.

After leaving Broadway I entered a region where asparagus, other vegetables and fruit are grown in large quantities.

The apple harvest being in full swing, Violet had a grand time, for wherever vendors sat behind their improvised stalls by the wayside, I bought her an apple or two which she munched with relish, her mouth slobbering and foaming for some time after.

By this time, although I allowed her to eat as much as she could hold, she had to a great extent recovered her " waist-line " ; in fact, she began to look almost elegant.

Strange to relate, although in former years I had done a great deal of riding, this was the first time in my life that I had ridden a mare.

In South America no cowboy ever uses a mare for riding purposes. In fact, if one were offered to a *gaucho* he would consider it a great insult, for only horses are ridden by these people, mares never.

In the pampas, the crown of virile dignity and " swank " is to be mounted on a fiery, half-tame (*redomon*) stallion, the proud rider adorning the animal with costly silver, or even gold trappings.

" The Crown " in Evesham was my next stopping place.

When I arrived, one section in a row of empty stalls was hastily " furnished," bedding, hay and oats being procured as if by magic.

The streets of the village (I beg your pardon, *town*, I mean) were festooned with garlands and flags, for on the morrow carnival was to be held, the proceeds of public collections going to a local hospital.

Already on the eve of the great day people made merry ; and early next morning the sound of church-bells and music heralded the beginnings of festivities.

Char-à-bancs filled with thirsty people from the " Black Country " began to arrive, men, women and even children having joined in this pilgrimage, which, as far as most of them were concerned, appeared to be merely an outing and a change of " pubs."

I was amused when I heard local people refer to these rowdy visitors as " foreigners."

Excitement ran high among local inhabitants. A stout and very humorous bank manager acted the part of carnival king to perfection, while the

" queen," obviously conscious of the envious and admiring glances of girls and young men, nervously did her best to act her exalted part.

Followed by their " court," including a skipping jester, the " king " and " queen " visited shops and bars, encouraging people to fill the money-boxes with which gaily-dressed maidens went through the streets and from door to door.

A gang of boisterous young fellows were the " highwaymen," whose duty it was to " hold up " cars and to obtain " ransom-money " from their occupants.

The *pièce de résistance* of the festivities was an ox which was being roasted over a fire in the market-place.

Surrounded by a dense crowd of spectators, the chef, fully aware of his great importance and authority, gave orders to his assistants who slowly turned the sizzling carcass which was fixed to a horizontal pole with a wheel at one end.

At noon the great and solemn moment arrived. The " king " and " queen," assisted by the mayor, who wore his insignia of office, gave the command for the massacre to begin, and soon after knives were busy cutting up the roasted ox, many willing hands making sandwiches which were sold to eager buyers.

Towards evening a procession passed through the streets, the gay and colourful *cortège* being headed by the local band. The day's festivities ended with a dance in the municipal hall where

"Violet" in front of her stable at "New House"

Cottage near Lyndhurst

New Forest

Old church near Timsbury

The South Downs

Wiltshire Cottage

Turning grass into locomotive power

Harvest near Ramsbury

Ancient and modern

Harvest, Oxford

Toll bridge near Sutton Courteney—

Worcester scenery

Broadway

Snowshill

old and young people made merry until long after midnight.

When the " pubs " closed, drivers and ticket-collectors of char-à-bancs helped some of the " foreigners " to take away friends who had imbibed so freely that they refused—or were unable—to move alone.

Finally, when the last " casualty " had been loaded, exhaust pipes snorted, and soon the wheeled monsters took their cargo of tired human beings into the night.

From Evesham I made a side-trip to Stratford-on-Avon, on the way passing through a little place called Bidford, locally nicknamed " Drunken Bidford."

I am unable to state whether or not so distinguished a name is justified, for, in passing I only saw one man who was lying by the wayside, obviously the worse for the wear and tear of elbow-bending.

Stratford-on-Avon would be a delightful place were it not for souvenir stalls, cafés, tea-shops and all that goes with modern tourist industry.

As I wandered through the streets, admiring some of the old houses and other sights of interest, I overheard the conversation of a boy and girl who were having a quarrel.

When the boy had finished a stream of rude remarks about the girl, she put her hands to her hips, and, looking at him over her shoulder, said with a saucy, defiant wink :

F

"O.K., big boy. Come up and see me some time."

Amused, and at the same time sickened by the thought that I had come to this place to hear echoes from Hollywood, I strolled towards the Shakespeare Memorial Theatre, wondering if anything the greatest of English poets has written is ever likely to sweep the world as has done the catch-phrase manufactured in Hollywood and recorded on celluloid by Mae West, in order to spread the *immortal* words among Christians in the four corners of the world.

If to-day an English-speaking person admitted to be unable to quote even one phrase out of Shakespeare's works, this would not cause much surprise, but if somebody claimed never to have heard about Mae West, this would be a bombshell, the effect of which even a Bateman would find difficult to depict.

Though the Memorial Theatre is a fine piece of modern architecture, I was, somehow, unable to connect it with Shakespeare.

On certain doors, leading off the dress-circle and stalls, I noticed the word " Gentlemen " written in chromium letters, whereas, on a door placed in the gallery for the same convenience, the letters G E N T L and E were omitted, leaving only the last three : M E N.

Supposing Shakespeare could come to life, and wished to see one of his own plays being acted in this theatre built in his memory I wonder if he would pay a few extra shillings for the privilege of sitting among GENTLEMEN, or if he would be satisfied to be among MEN up in the " gods " ?

From Stratford I went on to Warwick where, having paid two shillings, I was allowed to join a flock of tourists, hikers, cyclists and other sightseers who—like so many sheep in a corral—waited until a few more joined them to make up a " lot " to be taken through the castle by a guide.

Wearing my unfashionable riding outfit, I mixed with the little crowd that would have added to the colour of a fancy-dress ball.

One or two buxom ladies in their hiker regalia— very short and dangerously tight-fitting " shorts "— held my attention (and breath) until the glare of an American's gaudy chequered suit made me turn in another direction.

Cyclists, a couple of saintly-looking parsons, motorists from Scotland, Wales and England, hundred-per-centers—obviously from Poland via New York, demi-mondanes, men from Castile, Rome, Paris and Berlin, all were thrown together in the little chattering League of Nations which made up our " lot."

Never in my life had I been herded along with sightseers, but although the novelty of the experience amused me, I hope it will be the last one of its kind.

The guide—a bald-headed fellow, blessed with the patience of Job—spoke with the monotonous voice of a tired priest chanting his fourth litany in a day.

Every now and again somebody interrupted his mechanical recital with a question, two rather good-looking American ladies being the keenest seekers of information, wishing to know all about the *dooke's* private life, or how much the painting by Van Dyck, or that one by *Velasqueeze* might be worth.

Tramping from one hall to another, halting to listen to the human gramophone who was our guide, we moved along slowly, like a grazing herd of milch-cows.

In the " Bogey Room " (reputed to be haunted) probably pleased because he was nearing the end of another " round," he actually became humorous.

With the superior smile of a hero, he told his keen listeners that although he often had to do night-duty, and in doing it had to pass through the " Bogey Room," he had never seen a ghost. To this he added with a naughty and meaning twinkle in his eye, that after a good dinner he was some-times apt to imagine all sorts of things, especially when woodwork happened to creak.

At this point my American friend of the gaudy-chequered suit laughed boisterously, at the same time digging me in the ribs with an elbow.

" Oh, boy ! You're tellin' me," he said, loud enough for everybody to hear. " Don't I know that phoney feelin' ? Why ? After a good dinner I've seen ghosts, red snakes, blue geese an' pink 'gators. I'm tellin' the cock-eyed world, an' I don't mean maybe ! "

Suddenly all eyes were fixed on the pair of us, some blazing with indignation and others twinkling with merriment, but those of the two parsons were raised to the ceiling, as if looking for a crack in the woodwork.

Probably owing to the redness of my sunburnt face, most people thought I had made this public confession ; and as I stood there, forcing a grin and perspiring with embarrassment, the American, between roars of laughter at his own joke, kept on digging me in the ribs, nearly knocking the wind out of me.

I felt greatly relieved when I was once more out in the open, and alone.

Having taken two or three photographs I hurried through the dusk of the massive castle gate, thinking about dungeons, torture and gallows.

On reaching the walls of the surrounding park I read a notice warning visitors that there was an extra charge of sixpence for the use of cameras.

Although I had not paid this fee I had not the least desire to return, so I slunk away like a poacher, hoping that my pictures would turn out well.

CHAPTER TEN

Shadows of the Duc D'Orleans—Worcester—
A Lunatic—Her Grace, the Bar-Maid—
The " Smithy "

ATTRACTED by the sight of hills in the far distance,
I decided to head for Wales.

Accordingly, on leaving Evesham, I chose a
quiet road which led in the direction of Worcester.
This road, I knew, led past Wood Norton, a beautiful private school, which is being run by an
ex-headmaster of mine.

The house—a veritable palace—and its
surrounding parks formerly had belonged to Lord
Coventry, and was purchased by the Duc d'Aumale,
son of Louis Philippe, and bequeathed to his Great-
nephew the Duc d'Orleans, claimant to the throne
of France as representative of the Bourbon dynasty.

Unfortunately, I arrived at Wood Norton during
the school holidays, finding the place deserted.

I was just riding past the magnificent " golden
gate," adorned with gilded hand-forged angels and
fleurs-de-lis, when Violet suddenly shied.

Before I knew what was happening she slipped and fell, but fortunately I instinctively put out a foot, and as she scrambled to her feet she lifted me with her, still seated in the saddle.

Being afflicted with a normal man's vanity, I was sorry that nobody was there to see this lucky bit of horsemanship.

Perhaps the sight of golden angels on the gate had been too much for Violet, or maybe she sensed the intrigues which had at one time gone on behind these portals.

Formerly, when the duke lived in this place, only people of royal blood were permitted to pass through this gate, other visitors and messengers having had to use another entrance.

Built on a terrace on the slope of a high hill, the palatial house commands a wonderful view of the beautiful country below.

At one time a vast area of land around Wood Norton had been fenced off, and wild boar, stags and other game roamed about to provide the duke with sport befitting the would-be occupant of a throne.

For further royal entertainment, the duke had commanded a regular zoological garden to be built near the house, but when the place was turned into a school, the section where polar bears had formerly been kept, was transformed into a fine open-air swimming bath.

The house would make a paradise for anybody afflicted with *manie de grandesse*, for wherever one looks there are crowns, fleur-de-lis, coats-of-arms and royal standards—even on the gutter-pipes and on the boiler in the cellar.

The ride to Worcester was pleasant, though uneventful, excepting when—whilst I had some bread and cheese at an inn—Violet amused herself chewing up the publican's favourite rose-bush.

On discovering the damage done to the plant, the man became very angry ; but luckily his wife was a horse-lover, and poured oil on the raging sea.

In Worcester I found an excellent stable, near which was an inn where I obtained quarters.

With a sinking feeling I telephoned to my publishers in London, for I knew that by this time the proofs of my next book-to-be must be ready. I was not surprised when I was told to stay in Worcester, to which place the pile of printed agony would be sent immediately.

Cursing myself for not having chosen rich parents, and therefore now paying the penalty, having to work for a living, I hung up the receiver and sulkily slouched across the road to the stables, attached to which was a blacksmith's shop, where I watched the " smithy " hammer horseshoes into shape, making sparks fly like those of an exploding rocket.

The sound of an anvil, the homely breathing of bellows and the crackling of glowing charcoal, together with the odour of burnt hoofs, soon cheered me up ; and when the blacksmith had finished his day's work I invited him to have a pint of beer with me.

Horseshoeing being an art which is apt to make a man very thirsty, my newly-made friend accepted my offer with pleasure, and soon we were leaning up against a counter, between gulps, and after having wiped the froth from our mouths with the backs of our hands, discussing hoofs and horseshoes.

Presently the innkeeper's wife came in, and whispered to us that a madman was sitting in an adjoining room.

Apparently, the stranger had arrived the day before ; and, having been taken for a commercial traveller, was given a room.

In the morning the maid was puzzled to find that curtains, table-cloths, sheets and blankets had been tied into knots, and that little bits of twisted-up paper were stuck or placed wherever she looked.

Coming down the stairs the strange guest had met the hostess, who was surprised on seeing him sharpen a razor on a strop, one end of which he held in his teeth. She graphically described how he had looked at her with an uncanny grin, saying that a razor was an excellent instrument for cutting throats.

However, the strange customer soon went out, leaving the startled woman, who thought that he merely had a peculiar sense of humour.

Towards evening the man returned, acting so singularly that it dawned on her that the mysterious guest was a lunatic.

We could not help smiling as we watched the poor fellow go through a series of most extraordinary antics, putting a pipe from one pocket into another, down his trousers, under his hat, and balancing it behind his ears.

In the meantime somebody had telephoned to the police, and soon two men—who, though they wore civilian clothes, could at once be recognised as policemen—entered the bar and ordered drinks.

The lunatic, taking no notice of anybody, continued going through many most extraordinary antics, playing with bits of paper, letters and photographs, every now and again talking to himself, laughing or cursing, in a voice which sounded hollow and uncanny.

When, among other things, he slowly produced a razor, I could not help noticing the eyes of the onlookers, for they suddenly bulged, and expressions of suppressed mirth gave way to looks of horror as muscles tightened and breaths were being held.

Fortunately, the lunatic soon replaced his toys into his pockets, and rose to leave the place quietly, like a normal person.

Later in the evening we heard that the poor man had tried to commit suicide, and that he had to be taken to a lunatic asylum.

That night the sole conversation in the bar was about lunatics, everybody telling or inventing yarns, which became more and more interesting as the pretty daughters of the house continued to hand pints of beer over the counter.

English barmaids are a national institution.

Like sailors, stud-grooms and farmers, they are born—not made—and are a race apart from all the others.

Pleasing to look at, good-humoured and yet strictly business-like, a good barmaid is an invaluable asset to the tap-room, where men assemble to forget the humdrum of daily life.

Like a confessor, she sympathetically listens to intimate tales of woe and tribulation, but without ever asking an indiscreet question, or repeating to human ears what she has heard.

Being a kind of bar-room shepherdess, she knows every member of her flock ; and although she is aware of the colour of all her sheep, she keeps this knowledge strictly to herself.

To be a barmaid requires a keen sense of humour and an ever-ready wit, as well as the faculty of being able to change a sunny smile into a sad expression of understanding sympathy.

Tact and firmness are among the many other qualifications necessary to carry out her often difficult extra duties, for if troubles arise she has to act as arbitrator, and often even as restorer of peace.

Judges sometimes show their personal feelings by making remarks which are intended to influence juries, but a barmaid must be above such failings of her learned friends of the bench.

The unwritten laws of *her* bar she will never allow to be treated with contempt ; and if a breaker of its traditions or peace refuses to listen to reason she must be firm and decided, and strong enough to eject the offender without offending him.

A stock of the latest stories, of course, is a great asset, but a knowledge of current and past sporting events, flexible political opinions, a thorough acquaintance with current happenings—from farmer Brown's triplets down to Giles's mare who has slipped her second colt, and an infinity of other subjects, must be at her busy finger-tips.

And last, but not least, the perfect barmaid must know how to flirt and pretend to be in love with any customer who happens to feel amorously inclined. Often she has to do this with several clients at the same time, but without exciting feelings of jealousy.

According to her victims' different inclinations and tastes, she must play up to them, perhaps at the same time attending to other patrons, or talk to the local butcher about the price of hogs.

Although the typical English barmaid in cities has—to a large extent—been replaced by Greta Garbos and other flickering stars, she has survived in the rural districts.

May she continue to shine for ever, and be, as her sisters of the past have been, an asset and credit to the land which has given them birth.

During my short forced stay in Worcester I gave Violet a daily canter, and when I was tired of using red ink on the proofs, I went to the blacksmith's shop for recreation and relaxation.

Twisting sentences into shape, looking for repetitions of words, printer's errors (always blame them), and all that goes with the final touches necessary to complete a book, is boring enough at any time, but when this has to be done in the midst of a delightful riding-tour, words fail to express how one feels about it.

Not only in Worcester, but wherever I came to a forge, I always watched the blacksmiths do their work.

Often I have sat for hours, following every movement as irons were being shaped into horse-shoes and fitted on, for this difficult art has always fascinated and interested me.

Stockbrokers, politicians, petrol, oil, steel and many other respected magnates of modern civilis-ation may strut their brief hour upon the stage of this world ; but a good horse-shoer, like a great artist, is a gift from heaven.

To my knowledge, nowhere in the world there exist as many benevolent and humane societies as flourish in England, where animals enjoy the protection they are entitled to.

However, some of the English animal-lovers are carried away by their zeal to such an extent that their kind hearts become cruel ones.

If you look at some of the pampered dogs, and remember feline " nocturnes," you will understand what I mean.

I love animals, but I hate some " animal lovers."

CHAPTER ELEVEN

*The Vexing Problem of Horseshoeing—
Invasion of Hop-Pickers—Gambling—Mr.
Longodds Puts His Teeth on a Horse—
Ghosts of the Past*

IN various blacksmiths' shops I had occasion to make an observation which may be of interest to societies which make it their laudable duty to prevent suffering among working horses.

The problem of shoeing our equine slaves has always been a difficult and vexing one. Even experts disagree on various points connected with this delicate art.

In order not to bore readers who take no interest in this subject I will not go into details, but here I must mention that some of the relatively well-paid inspectors do not qualify for the positions they hold.

I have seen horses whose hoofs were in shocking condition ; and yet the unfortunate brutes were being worked every day, and blacksmiths were expected to shoe them when it was impossible to drive nails into the diseased hoofs without causing intense suffering.

94

How can a local ex-policeman be expected to know horses and their many ailments ; and is he likely to interfere with personal friends who often happen to be the owners of overworked, half-crippled horses ?

Surely old blacksmiths would make ideal inspectors, provided they were sent to parts of the country where they are strangers.

True, this would involve a certain amount of travelling and expense, but the money would not be spent in vain, as happens in some cases under the present system of inspection.

* * * * *

The hop harvest was about to begin in Worcestershire. Gipsies, people from the vicinity, and others from the industrial districts flocked through Worcester on their way to the hop-plantations.

As far as most members of this invading army were concerned, hop-picking seemed to be an excuse to get out into the fresh air, to meet people, and to spend a few merry days.

When I watched some of these poorly-clad pilgrims who filled the bar, I was amazed to see how much money they spent.

Round after round of whisky, gin and expensive stout was ordered, the drinks acting as fuel to keep up conversations about horse-racing, greyhounds and football pools.

To one like myself, who is only interested in

racing and games as sports, the amount of gambling done in England is surprising.

Throughout the year certain newspapers have special daily racing editions, which sell like the proverbial hot cakes.

Race meetings and greyhound tracks attract enormous crowds, who always seem to have money for a " flutter," even though they talk about hard times, and stint themselves as far as the first necessaries of life are concerned.

Servants, labourers and other members of the " lower " classes who are unable to go to race-meetings, place their bets with street bookmakers, while better-to-do citizens of the " upper " classes communicate with their " agents," making their bets by mail or over the telephone.

Though betting in public-houses is illegal, it is as common and easy as is the buying and selling of newspapers.

Despite the fact that I have never had a bet of even a farthing, off or on an English race-track, I know at least half a dozen London street " bookies," who seem to be doing a roaring trade under the very nose of the police.

Knowing nothing about the ways and wherefores of legal matters, I am at a loss to understand why betting in the streets should be illegal when big firms of bookmakers are allowed to take bets in their sumptuous offices, which—with their telephone exchanges, clerks and imposing rows of files—look like banks.

Snowshill

Evesham preparing the ox

Warwick Castle

Cottage near Knightwick (Worcester)
(Note old ornamental chimney-pots)

Stratford-on-Avon

Evesham—The Mayor arriving

Old English Forge in Worcester

Hop Pickers (Worcester)

Hop Harvest near Worcester

Llangollen, Plas Newydd (House of Old Ladies)

Plas Newydd

"Violet" eating her way into Wales

Two personal acquaintances of mine happen to be what Americans call " big shots " in this line of business, so I am able to describe their offices from personal observation.

Bookmakers, " punters " and betting being the subject, reminds me of a pathetic though humorous episode which happened in London recently. Incredible as the story may sound, I vouch for its truth, though, naturally, I refrain from giving the real names of my heroes.

Mr. Longodds has been a gambler ever since he came to the conclusion that money is intended to circulate.

Being the only son of an old county family he was sent to the best schools, for his parents were determined that, even if nothing else, their son must become a " gentleman."

On leaving " varsity "—where he had chiefly studied " form-books," odds and chances—young Mr. Longodds was firmly convinced that a gentleman had to be a fool to work for his living when race-meetings were being held practically every day, and therefore he soon became a familiar figure among the *habitués* on race-courses all over the United Kingdom.

In the company of lords and ladies he could be seen strutting about the enclosures reserved for the *élite* ; and if he passed trainers, jockeys or bookmakers, they respectfully doffed their caps or hats, smiling with pride if Mr. Longodds acknowledged their greetings.

97

During cold, wet and foggy winters our lion of the racing world went to Monte Carlo, where, for a change, he played baccarat and roulette.

Years passed. Sometimes Dame Fortune smiled on our hero—but this only when a wealthy relative died.

The three fortunes left to him had gone into the coffers of casinos and bookmakers, who referred to Mr. Longodds as one of the finest " sportsmen " the English turf had ever known.

By degrees our friend came to the end of his resources. A frantic search and study of his family " form-book " revealed the distressing fact that the only remaining " products " were poor, or impossible to handle. Thus, by degrees, our hero came down in life, until, finally, he became an inmate of a London workhouse.

On rare occasions, when he managed to borrow or otherwise raise a few shillings, he had a " flutter " on a " dead certainty " ; but invariably he overlooked two or three horses who upset the apple-cart by finishing ahead of his fancy.

One day, glancing through a newspaper, he saw that one of his special fancies—a horse which simply could not lose—was quoted at 20 to 1.

This was too much for Mr. Longodds, who had visions of a bright and gay future as he strode through the streets of London on his way to a bookmaker he had dealt with in former years.

Surprised to see his old customer appear, the " bookie " eyed him like a Harley Street specialist looking at a prospective patient. After formal greetings and enquiries as to health, but carefully avoiding the topic of prosperity, the bookmaker rubbed his hands and asked what he could do for his old client.

Ten pounds on the 20 to 1 would have been a surprisingly small bet for Mr. Longodds in the good old days, but now it almost staggered the book-maker, who forced a conversation while waiting for the cash to be placed on his desk.

Finally, when the " bookie " had screwed up sufficient courage, he coughed once or twice and then asked our hero for the money.

Explaining that he had come down to the last " bean," Mr. Longodds then offered to give a guarantee, whereupon he took from his mouth a beautiful set of false teeth—the last testimonial of old prosperous days.

In due time the race was run, and when the evening papers announced the result, our un-fortunate " punter " rubbed his chin, which—owing to the fact that its owner's teeth were in the book-maker's safe—now nearly touched the nose.

The next few days were trying ones for poor Mr. Longodds, for his now sore gums made it impossible for him to eat anything harder than workhouse porridge, soup and other " slops."

Soon the unlucky man's clothes began to hang down like the sails of an old windjammer in a calm, and a ravenous appetite tormented him like rats nibbling at his intestines.

One day, whilst out walking, Mr. Longodds happened to meet an old friend who felt so sorry for him that he gave him two pounds.

Rushing to the first telephone booth our hero rang up the bookmaker and invited him to have dinner in a certain restaurant.

Hearing the excited voice at the other end of the line, the man of finance—probably suspecting that his old client had inherited another fortune—immediately accepted the invitation.

" By the way," Mr. Longodds said before hanging up the receiver, " please don't forget to bring my teeth. I need them badly."

That night, seated in a restaurant, the hero of this true story was much too busy devouring a huge steak and other savour dishes to talk to the flabbergasted bookmaker, who looked on like a child watching a sword-swallower perform his tricks.

When Mr. Longodds could eat no more, he conversed for a while over a *café-noir* and cognac ; and when his cigar had burnt down until it was impossible to have another puff without burning his lips, he took the teeth from his mouth and handed them back to the bookmaker, in whose safe they are still being kept while I am writing this story.

* * * * *

So much for gambling. Now back to Worcester, where, in the meantime, I had finished correcting the proofs of my book.

Surrounded by a group of newly-made friends,
I saddled up, and when farewells had been said
I mounted, and soon was on my way towards
Wales.

About nine miles out of Worcester I halted in a
little place called Knightwick, where the hop
harvest was in full swing.

It was very interesting to watch the army of
pickers at work, men, women and children, chattering and joking as they filled baskets with
cone-shaped hops.

Two char-à-bancs, filled with friends of
hop-pickers who had come from the " Black
Country," arrived, the merry and noisy visitors
soon joining in the fun, helping the workers in
their task until evening, when they would return
home, after having spent an enjoyable day in the
open.

The only people who took their work seriously,
were the gipsies, who kept apart from the others,
working fast and quietly, and in comparative
silence.

Many years ago I had been a private tutor to
two boys whose parents owned a fine old estate
near Knightwick, so I decided to visit the place
once more.

As I passed the lodge and entered the drive, I
remembered some of the stately old trees which,
like the winding river Teme, looked exactly as they
had done years ago.

There was the spot where Jackie had shot his

first rabbit ; over yonder the field where I had been lucky to escape meeting with a serious shooting accident ; and below me, just visible through the tops of tall trees, I caught a glimpse of the river-bank, off which we used to dive to swim in the clear cool water.

Continuing along the winding drive, I noticed that it was partly overgrown with grass and moss ; and when I came to a gate I found it securely fastened with a thick rusty chain and a padlock, which had apparently not been opened for a long time.

Climbing over the corroded gate, on which only remained a few peeling chips of old paint, I slowly followed along the drive afoot until I came to the moat, which I remembered so well.

The tiny island on it now looked like a veritable jungle, and its surrounding waters were greenish-black, with a dense mass of weed and other aquatic plants.

On the opposite side of the moat I saw the garden which, though more or less tended, looked forlorn as a solitary bunch of beautiful flowers would if it were placed in the archæological section of a museum.

Looking round the curve of the moat I then saw W. Court, the house whose memory had some-times haunted me when I was in South American forests or high up in the loneliness of the snow-swept Andes.

Like eyelids closed in mourning, shutters hid the

windows of the house ; and the sad cooing of a wood-pigeon contrasted strangely with the joyful song of birds in the trees.

Having climbed over a second gate, which was also fastened with a chain and a rusty padlock, I hesitatingly continued my walk along the drive until I halted at the main entrance door of the big house.

Though some instinct told me that I would get no response, I rang the bell, and against my expect-ation, listened for approaching footsteps from within.

After a while, driven by curiosity, I explored the back of the house and the stable-yard, where weeds and moss grew between the cobble-stones, and then, feeling like an intruder, I hurried towards the old, tiny church which stands close by.

As I pushed open the heavy, worm-eaten oak door, it creaked on its hinges, making me hesitate before penetrating into the church's gloomy interior, where my gingerly footsteps sounded like the pounding of hoofs.

Looking at the altar, lectern, pulpit and pews, with their worn Bibles and prayer-books, I had visions of the past.

First faintly, then clearer and clearer, I imagined seeing the small congregation, listening to the rector who delivered a sermon.

Standing erect, his powerful shoulders showing to full advantage in the robes he wore, the preacher spoke slowly and clearly, every now and again accentuating a statement by slightly lowering or raising his handsome white head, whilst his clear, penetrating, though kindly eyes, wandered along the rows of faces looking up to him.

In order not to disturb the assembly of pious ghosts, I tiptoed towards the door, which I gently closed behind me.

Guided by curiosity I then slowly wandered through the churchyard, examining the few grave-stones which appeared to be new, the old ones being covered with moss and chipped, stained or peeling with age.

Having read and re-read the inscription on a white marble cross, I could hardly believe that the mortal remains of Sir R. lay buried beneath it, for I remembered my old friend so well that I felt as if he were standing by my side, reading and thinking with me.

A sudden gust of wind and the rustling of leaves brought me back to reality, whereupon, without turning to look back, I hastily retraced my steps towards the place where I had left Violet who—by this time—surely must be impatiently waiting for me, and soon W. Court, its remote and immed-iate past, melted into one memory.

CHAPTER TWELVE

Gossipers Beware ! — Ludlow — Wales —
English Grumblings of Contentment—Powis
Castle — National Games — Cricket, The
" King of Games "

RIDING over beautiful hills from where I had
magnificent views, I proceeded in the direction
of Leominster. (Locally pronounced *Lemster*).

On the outskirts of a hamlet near the top of a
hill, a few miles from Knightwick, I came to one
of the most picturesque old English forges I have
seen.

Whenever I found a spot of beauty or interest, I
dropped my South American split reins, slid off the
mare, and let her graze whilst I went to have a look
round.

There was no need to tie up Violet, for she
would never have left a spot so long as there was
something green to nibble—leaves off bushes or
hedges, and even low-hanging twigs of trees being
all the same to her.

In Lancashire they have a word denoting a horse

which is a good feeder, the local adjective for such an animal being " dawsome."

By this time the mare had learnt to avoid stepping on the long raw-hide reins, which she dragged along by throwing up her head before taking two or three steps. Invariably, she slowly moved towards the place where I happened to be, and on reaching me sniffed and nuzzled one of my pockets she knew very well, hoping she would receive a lump of sugar or some other titbit. Sometimes, when she was disappointed, she rubbed her velvety nose against me, or impatiently butted me with her broad forehead, at the same time nickering somewhere deep down in her glossy throat.

In one of the churches in Leominster is kept the last " dipping-chair " used in England.

Fixed to long poles this chair was formerly used to give evil-tongued women a good " ducking " in the river ; a form of punishment which would still be very effective to-day, not only for women, as in the " good old days," but also for some of the " gentlemen " who frequently assemble in clubs to discuss the " conquests " they have—or have not—made.

Unable to find quiet lanes or open country, I was obliged to follow alongside the main road which led towards Ludlow, where I found a good stable in a quaint little inn built on the high rocks alongside the old stone bridge (Ludford Bridge) which leads into the town, situated on the opposite side of the river Teme.

There being a great deal of interest to see in Ludlow, I decided to stay there next day in order to visit the castle and to have a good look at the beautiful Tudor houses and other buildings of note.

In the evening, sitting out on a little garden terrace in front of the inn, I listened to the murmur of the waters below me, at the same time dreamily looking at the outline of the walls and towers of the castle, high up on a hill on the other side of the river.

Below me, an angler was slowly wading in the shallow water, casting his fly, whilst near him a few snow-white swans were lazily floating about, arranging their feathers, or with heads under water, searching for food.

Gazing at the silhouette of the castle, I made mental pictures of what I imagined it must have looked like shortly after the Norman Conquest.— Past glories, deeds of valour and daring, victories, defeats, intrigues, joys, sufferings, loves, hatreds, and visions of armies paraded before my mind's eye until the last after-glow of red had faded in the western horizon, the silhouette of the castle gradually blending into one with the twinkling stars and the dark-purple sky of a moonless summer's night.

When I left Ludlow, Violet, who had not wasted her time in the stable, was so lazy that I dismounted to cut a little hazel stick in a hedge.

As I used neither a whip nor spurs, she had not

taken the slightest notice of my heels, with which I had thumped her bulging flanks ; but when I again mounted, and she saw the stick through the corner of an eye, she immediately moved like a real " goer."

Soon, however, with the contempt bred by familiarity, she became so used to the sight of the stick that I had to use it mildly, but when she had become accustomed to feeling it on one side I had to change it over to my other hand.

This she resented strongly at first, the immediate result being that she trotted along with snorts of protest at such cunning and unfair tactics.

Finding that the nasty little stick hurt no more on the off side than it had done on the near, she again settled down to her sluggish pace, every now and again stopping to snatch a mouthful of grass.

Raising the stick slowly until it was behind her sturdy neck, and thus hidden from her sly backward glances, I would then suddenly give her a flick on the left or right flank—a most aggravating and disconcerting trick, which, however, had the desired effect.

Whilst trotting along she constantly glanced back at me with foxy eyes, wondering where the stick might be. Whenever she tried to slow down, I only had to wag it from side to side to make her go so fast that she even tried to gallop.

When the time arrived to have our periodical short rest, I dismounted to let her nibble a little grass while I sat down to smoke a cigarette.

My equine companion had developed a habit of always grazing towards me, and somehow, wherever I happened to sit, she seemed to think that the grass under me was the best ; and therefore I was constantly being pushed out of the way.

On this occasion I had laid down my little stick beside me, determined to continue my game with it if the mare would not behave better after this short rest.

Suddenly, I heard a particularly loud crunching noise in Violet's mouth, and turning round to see what she was doing, I saw her devour my hazel stick which, judging by the expression in her eyes, seemed to give her great joy.

Laughing at the unexpected end of my game, I patted the mare's neck, for she had won. When I mounted to proceed I did it without a stick, for, after all, this was a holiday, and Violet, like myself, must have days when she feels lazy and slack, and therefore wants to take things easy.

I was glad to be in rural districts once more. Whenever it was possible, I followed minor roads and lanes, which I found by consulting farmers or my maps.

Soon I came to lovely hilly country where I occasionally met people driving in two-wheeled traps, which were being pulled by sturdy little ponies who climbed up steep inclines with the ease of mountain goats. Wonderful creatures some of these ponies are.

I spent a most entertaining evening in Bishop's

Castle, where the mare was very happy in the stables attached to a small hotel.

As usual, I soon made friends with people who wanted to hear all about my recent travels. Every now and again I had to go to the stable to show them Violet, who would be looked over by critical eyes.

What always interested me most were the conversations held over pints of beer.

Putting it in general terms, the average Englishman is a very happy person ; in fact, so happy that he finds cheer in grumbling.

Wherever English people live together, be it in small rural communities, in the army, or even on luxurious transatlantic liners, something must be radically wrong if they do not grumble about things, such as comforts, food, discipline, or for the want of anything else, about the weather—which is either too hot, cold, dry, wet or variable.

Farmers, as far as my experience goes, are England's champion grumblers.

If I tried to put down in writing the endless and extraordinary grievances I have heard, they would fill a thick and most entertaining volume.

The funny part about all this is that when an Englishman comes to the end of a bout of grumbling, he laughs about it all, and the only thing that really annoys him is that he cannot think of any other grievance.

A few miles out of Bishop's Castle I came to a stone which marks the Welsh border where, in order to celebrate so important an event, I dismounted to smoke a cigarette. Whilst I took things easy, Violet did the same, taking advantage to eat her way into Wales.

As I was looking around for a good subject to photograph, I saw a rabbit who was in the middle of the road, apparently observing me with curiosity.

A little later, when I was once more in the saddle and slowly approached the rabbit, I noticed that he tried to struggle out of my way, but was unable to move.

On reaching the frightened little animal I found that both its hind-legs were broken. Apparently a car had run over the poor little chap, whom I reluctantly put out of his misery.

Riding along motor roads, I was often surprised at the number of dead birds and other little animals which lay by the wayside. Obviously they had been struck by passing cars.

Near Welshpool I had a delightful ride through the park surrounding Powys Castle. I do not know if I was trespassing, but even if I did, I enjoyed the exquisite beauty of its scenery.

High up, on the very top of a wooded hill, stands the castle, from where one has magnificent views of the green hilly country below.

In a big clearing, flanked by stately old trees, grazed or rested many deer, which completed as enchanting a picture as ever I have seen.

Farther down, on a flat piece of ground which was carpeted with well-kept turf, two local teams played a cricket-match, the tiny white figures of the players showing up well against the dark and light-green stripes where a mowing-machine had passed over the field.

Having seen enough of the park, I slowly rode down a winding road, and when I had found a spot where the grass looked good, I let the mare graze, whilst I went to watch the cricketers at play.

England's national games—taking them in their order of popularity—are, Association football, cricket and Rugby football.

During recent years, some people who consider themselves to belong to the " better " class, have labelled " soccer " as the game for " common " people.

Owing to the fact that the masses are poor— and therefore " common "—they naturally play the cheapest game.

All that is needed to play " soccer " is a ball (or even rags tied together) and a patch of ground— rough or smooth, it makes little difference to enthusiasts. Coats, tin cans, hats or other objects can be made to take the place of goal-posts.

Owing to the popularity the game enjoys, masses of professional teams flourish, players being bought and transferred from one club to another.

Clubs belonging to the Association Football League are really powerful commercial enterprises which, according to the profits they make, pay dividends to shareholders who, perhaps, have never kicked a football in their lives.

As far as professional football is concerned, the old competitive spirit is dead, for with the system of purchase and transfer of players, it is rare to-day to see a native play for his home town.

Players from Scotland, Wales and Ireland, or from different parts of England, defend the colours of London teams ; perhaps a year later to be transferred to another town or city, where a club requires their services.

However, in spite of this, " fans " have their favourite teams, which they support with yells and money paid for admission.

" Rugger " is rapidly gaining ground, but I do not think the game is ever likely to become as popular with the masses as " soccer " is to-day.

As far as most Englishmen are concerned, cricket, in their opinion, is the " king of games."

To play this scientific game properly the following necessaries are required : white buckskin boots with spikes, carefully-creased white flannel trousers, a white shirt, a bat, pads and gloves. Caps and their colours are optional, but old school blazers, with imposing crests on the breast-pockets, are great and enviable social assets.

Probably the most important requisite is the field or ground, which requires the attention and care of artists in order to keep it in perfect condition.

This in itself supplies members of cricket clubs with unlimited material for scientific conversations which often last for hours as enthusiasts gravely

H

wander over the field, identifying pernicious weeds, carefully burrowing for grubs, worms or insects, looking for bumps, soft or hard patches, and a thousand other important details, which are discussed solemnly and at length.

Again bats are examined, admired or criticised, their good points or flaws being debated with seriousness, as if the fate of the Empire depended on them.

The technicalities of the rules governing the game are so intricate and complicated that—during spare moments, especially over drinks—enthusiasts invent peculiar situations and happenings in imaginary matches, asking their listeners whether or not the player of their example would be " out."

For the benefit of odd readers who know little or nothing about this extraordinary game, I must here mention that " out " really means a batsman going back into the gloom of the pavilion. Therefore, in cricket language, " out " really means " in."

Sometimes, when opinions as to the interpretation of rules are so divided that endless correspondences fill newspapers, it is decided, for a final verdict, to appeal to a mysterious body called the M.C.C. (Roman numerals standing for one thousand two hundred experts, I presume.) As far as I am able to make out, even the opinions of these twelve hundred high priests in the Valhalla of cricket are often divided on certain technical points connected with the game, the M.C.C., as a body, not being able to fall into line. Hence, I surmise, originated the famous controversy over "body-line."

In former years, before inaptitude forced me to give up the game, I had had fond visions of becoming a star in first-class cricket.

To one like myself who is not a good bowler, and who is not blessed with the superhuman patience which is required to make a successful batsman, the "king of games" merely consists of putting on pads, slowly—and in a dignified manner—walk out to the wicket, and then back to the pavilion, while, perhaps, two or three mummy-like spectators might try to cheer me up with half-whispered remarks such as, "Bad luck, sir," or "Hard lines, sir."

Fielding I usually found to be as trying as batting (which meant sitting near the sleepy scorers).

"Fielding" means standing out somewhere in the field and waiting until six balls have been delivered from one end, and then walking miles to another spot, where one again waits until, perhaps, one's dreams are disturbed by a call "over!" which comes from one of the two umpires, who look like surgeons in full working regalia.

Often, when I was just about to doze off, the silence was suddenly broken by blood-curdling war-whoops, which came from my suddenly excited team-mates, and as I looked up I would see a ball whizz past me.

Chasing after it like a greyhound behind a hare, I usually caught it after it had hit the fence, a hedge or a spectator's foot, and when I threw the ball back to the bowler I could see the umpire signal to one of the scorers, who immediately woke up.

Rising from his comfortable seat he would then go over to the score-board and hang up a large 4, while the spectators gravely clapped their hands—and my team-mates muttered words I was fortunate not to be able to hear.

Although, maybe, the game had been in progress for well over half an hour, and I had done the only running, one of our opponents had—without even attempting to run—scored four runs.

This, like many other details connected with the game, is a highly technical point, for in cricket the quickest scorer of runs is the batsman who does the least running. His opponents in the field are expected to do this for him.

Before passing on to another subject I would like to give just a few more explanations about the extraordinary game, hoping it will help readers who are not familiar with cricket to understand a little about the " king of games."

One " over " consists of six times over bowling from one end of the " wicket " to the other, and, as far as the batsmen are concerned, of hitting, or trying to hit the ball all over, or clean out of the field.

" Stumped " means when two little sticks, called " bails "—resting horizontally on three vertical sticks stuck into the ground—are knocked off by the " wicket-keeper," who, when in a crouching position, is hardly visible behind the huge pads which protect his legs. This important player lurks behind the symmetrically-arranged sticks with the " bails " on them. Unlike other keepers, the wicket-keeper does everything within his power to " break " the sticks in his charge.

When, under certain technical circumstances, a batsman is " bailed out," as it were, in reality he is sent into the pavilion.

A " leg-bye " is a run scored by means of a batsman's legs when the hard ball has glanced off one or both of them without breaking the wicket.

" Leg-theory " is a cunning practice of bowlers who know that most men act cautiously when threatened with pain.

" Out-field " is a man who is hardly out in the field, but usually to be seen standing on its very edge.

" Slips " are often tall men who try to make batsmen look small.

" Point " is a player who is placed so close to the batsmen that he often does not see the point why he should be placed where he cannot see the ball whizz past him.

" Cover " and " extra cover " are men who stand somewhere out in the field enjoying a sleep in the sunshine or rain.

The spectators can be classified in two categories : those who sleepily observe the movements of the white-clad figures in the field, and if there happens to be some new-mown hay in the vicinity, enjoy its smell or get hay fever, and the others who spend their time standing or sitting where stimulant refreshments are served. The score-board and occasionally a " skied " ball are the only things to remind members of the latter category that cricket is being played, but when, at long intervals, applause interrupts their academic conversations, they join in heartily, immediately after to produce pencils and score-cards on which to make new entries to be handed down to posterity. And so, as far as these happy enthusiasts are concerned, the game goes on until stumps are drawn, whereafter, to make it a perfect day, the same is done to a few more corks.

CHAPTER THIRTEEN

Worship and a Country Service—Lack of
Imagination—English Food—Llangollen—
Wrexham

I RARELY travelled on Sundays. Besides giving
the mare a rest, I found pleasure in reading or
aimlessly loafing about, watching people who did
the same.

In rural districts Sundays are so dull and boring
that I always felt slack and tired on Monday
mornings, for nothing wears a normal person down
more, physically and mentally, than complete
inactivity.

Once, having been invited by a local rector, I
went to his church.

The small congregation consisted chiefly of
villagers, a few farmers and their wives, all of
whom were dressed in their Sunday " best " and
looking stiff, as if they were clad in armour.

When half the pews in the little church were
filled with rigidly sitting people, there was suddenly
a rustle which could be heard above the mournful

gurgling of the organ's *vox humana*, which seemed to be the organist's favourite stop.

Presently, two figures which might have come out of an old novel, strode up the aisle, all eyes following them until they were seated in one of the front pews where the verger, with a blush of humility and pride, pushed the prayer-cushions into position, whereupon he squirmed away, self-consciously rubbing his hands, while a facial expression of shyness distorted his features, making his eyes resemble those of a fried fish.

A local store-keeper who happened to be my neighbour, leaned towards me, and, without taking his eyes off the two people in the front pew, whispered into my ear that the latest arrivals were Lord and Lady X.

Although this information helped me but little, I nodded knowingly, at the same time pretending to be surprised by raising my eyebrows, whereupon a girl, who just then happened to look towards me, blushed and turned away quickly to open her prayer-book.

Suddenly the organist—whose semi-bald head reminded me of paintings representing saints— struck up a tune which sounded like a march. Almost at the same instant a curtain was drawn aside, whereupon a procession, headed by a boy who carried a cross, slowly and awkwardly waddled, tramped and shuffled in from the vestry.

Standing up, like the rest of the congregation, I watched the choir-boys in their cassocks and surplices (which reminded me of old-fashioned night-shirts) slowly walk as if they were on ice.

Looking down shyly, they appeared to be looking at their clumsy boots, which protruded from under cassocks with every stride.

Judging by the appearance of the youngsters' carefully parted hair, water had been liberally applied, but even this had not tamed down some of the rebellious tufts which made two or three heads look as if they grew one or several horns.

Some of the choir-boys' faces had been soaped and scrubbed so well that they glowed and shone, skins on chubby cheeks being so tight that they threatened to burst.

Behind the two files of boys followed the men, the tall, Herculean village blacksmith dwarfing the rest of the little procession, at the end of which came the thin, pale-faced vicar, who immediately smiled and slightly bowed towards the two demi-gods in the front pew.

When the procession had filed into the choir-stalls, the service began according to the stereotyped routine, the congregation standing, sitting or kneeling like well-drilled soldiers, murmuring prayers, chanting responses, racing through the Psalms (in spite of the organist's frantic efforts to check the stampede), then, in contrast, to drag behind the organ in singing hymns, the poor man at the keyboard swaying forwards and backwards trying to hasten the tempo, his movements suggesting the pulling of a heavy cart.

Then we listened to a special rendering by the choir, the blacksmith, vicar and an angelic choir-boy singing the solos.

The sermon, contrary to warnings I had been given before entering the church, fortunately, was very short. This, I later found out, was due to the fact that the vicar's set of false teeth had been sent to London for repairs.

At long last, after two brass plates, covered with embroidered purple cloths, had been handed along the rows of worshippers—who at the time were singing the final hymn—two vergers took the collection up to the altar, where the vicar received it.

The final " Amen " having been chanted, the organist pulled out all the stops, suddenly to start playing as lively a " voluntary " as he dare, where-upon the choir-boys filed out of their pews so quickly that two would have bolted had it not been for the strong arm of the village blacksmith, who pulled them back in time.

The congregation respectfully waited until Lord and Lady X had strutted out, and then, accompanied by the music of the organ, the rest of us shuffled out into the sunshine, where, standing in little groups, everybody's eyes were fixed on his lordship and his worthy wife, who, after having had a short conversation with the bowing and beaming vicar, rolled away in their glistening car.

Like a frisky colt let loose, one of the choir-boys forgot himself to such an extent that he leap-frogged over an old tombstone, having to be severely reprimanded by the vicar.

By degrees the little groups of chatting people drifted down the gravel path towards the church-yard gate, from where they slowly scattered in different directions.

Later, among the men assembled in the tap-room of my inn, I recognised two or three members of the choir.

As I watched them dip their moustaches in the frothy beer, and I listened to their grunts of contentment between gulps, my heart went out to these brave singers, who fully deserved every drop they drank to loosen their over-worked vocal cords. Standing in groups, or wandering about like lost sheep, seem to be the only Sunday pastimes for men in the country.

Frequently, however, one sees amorous couples making love alongside public thoroughfares, the lovers being quite undisturbed by the glances, laughter and tittering of passers-by.

Anybody who has walked through London parks, especially when the weather happens to be warm and fine, will have noticed this same indifference of flirting couples who are lying about everywhere, often almost indecently, quite indifferent to the crowds of people who walk past, looking at them. Casual observers are either amused or shocked at this love-making in public and in broad daylight, but when one considers the mentality of these " lovers," one comes to the conclusion that they must lack even the faintest trace of imagination.

To be an artist an individual must be gifted (or is it cursed ?) with imagination.

I am afraid that in this respect Nature has not affected (or afflicted) the rank and file of Englishmen, who are unable to take an interest in matters connected with the abstract.

Even as far as food is concerned, the masses in England refuse to appreciate the culinary art, being happy and satisfied with the plainest roast or boiled food.

In defence of typical English dishes, however, I must admit that they are wholesome and healthy and, above all, that it is difficult to eat more of them than is necessary to satisfy one's appetite !

Eggs and bacon, marmalade, toast, tea, hot or cold roast beef (later re-edited as " cottage pudding " or " shepherd's pie," or disguised as mince, etc., etc.), Yorkshire and Sussex pudding (or is it Norfolk dumpling ?), roast or boiled mutton, pork or beef sausages, fried fish, steak, fried onions and " chips," half a dozen different puddings, pickles, cakes, bread, butter and three or four simple sauces are sufficient variety of food to keep most Englishmen happy for life.

Of course, labourers must have their beer and tobacco ; and woe to the government which would dare to make the price of these " necessaries " of life prohibitive.

The passing of a bill or budget which would financially place them beyond the reach of the masses, I really believe would lead to riots, bloodshed or even civil war, which otherwise is inconceivable among the tranquil, good-natured and disciplined Britons who are not afflicted with the restless temperament typical of artistic people, who often become so inartistic and unphilosophical that they suddenly revert to such primitive and concrete methods as the breaking of heads of their fellow-citizens.

It may be correct to argue that Man only learns with hard knocks, but when sorrows and tribulations can be forgotten by just gently tapping on a counter, and for a few pennies receive a pint of " inspiration," I wonder whether, perhaps, the tap is not the best way to become some kind of artist, philosopher, statesman, strong man or world-reformer, while, temporarily, King Bacchus speaks.

Keeping off the main roads, even if this meant making detours, I passed through Oswestry, and from there on to Llangollen—one of the quaintest places I stopped at on the whole ride.

Situated in a deep, green valley among high hills, there is something restful, and yet impressive, about Llangollen, where I spent a day looking at some of the old houses, the finest and most remarkable among them being Plas Newydd (House of Old Ladies).

Its elaborately carved black beams, windows, porches and doors, together with the beautiful garden and stately glen, make it a spot I shall always remember with delight.

When I close my eyes, and memory takes me back into the coolness of the glen, I can hear the soft murmuring of the tiny stream which flows along its bottom. I can see the crystal-clear water wind its way downwards among moss-covered stones, forming miniature waterfalls and whirlpools which gurgle and bubble, whilst a soft breeze rustles the leaves of the high trees which form a veritable roof overhead.

Carried away by imagination, I have visions of fairies dancing on patches of moss, and around the ivy-covered tree-trunks, whilst—like shifting spotlights—flickering sunbeams penetrate through the dense light green foliage above.

Following winding foot-paths, I slowly wander over tiny bridges—the stones of which are hardly visible under moss and ivy. At one of the old wells I drink deeply, as if I had discovered the Fount of Youth, rumours about the existence of which had driven brave Spanish *conquistadores* of old into the forbidding depths of South American jungles.

I like to think that the spirits of the two old ladies of Llangollen continue to wander in their worldly paradise, that fairies, elves and gnomes dance for them, whilst—side by side—they sit watching their graceful display which, I hope, will continue so long as the soft, silvery-blue light of the moon shines down on Plas Newydd.

Leaving this beautiful spot, I crossed the old stone bridge which spans the river, and started a long climb up a high hill, at the summit of which are the ruins of " Crow Castle."

When, puffing and panting, I stood on its crumbling walls, I was fully rewarded for the efforts I had made to reach the place, for the panorama I beheld was really magnificent.

Looking down into the valley, I saw Llangollen at my feet, the houses looking like tea-leaves in an empty cup.

Through the opening of the valley, towards the east, I had a glimpse of the rolling country beyond, and when I turned west, north and south, I saw nothing but hills, green valleys and mountains, which faded away at the hazy horizon, typical of a perfect summer's day.

Remembering that Violet was waiting for me, I started the descent into the valley. Running, jumping over stones, and sliding where the turf was slippery, I hurried down the steep slopes like an Andean Indian ; and when the shadows of evening were lengthening I jogged towards Wrexham.

The villages through which I passed were dismal and depressing, for now I was in a colliery district.

At the doors of the small, grimy stone houses stood men and women who looked as dismal as their habitations. On open patches of ground and in gloomy alleys played miserably-clad children, whose laughter and joyous shouts contrasted strangely with the dreary surroundings.

In the distance, ahead of me, a curtain of smoke

hung over the horizon, as if warning me to keep out of the regions beyond.

Every now and again I saw derelict factories and abandoned pits—sad testimonies of former times of commercial prosperity.

Nearing Wrexham, I passed near by the Gresford colliery, little dreaming that within a few days it would be the scene of one of the most appalling mining disasters.

As I approached the road which leads to the pit, a shift had just come off duty, and numerous miners shuffled home in their heavy clogs, the sound of which made the mare snort and look about nervously.

One of the men beckoned to me to stop, and presently he came to pet Violet, at the same time giving her an apple he had produced out of one of his pockets.

After a short conversation with this man, I continued my now short journey towards Wrexham, where I soon found a good stable and a comfortable inn.

A few days later, when I read about the disaster in the Gresford pit, I felt the shock all the more because I had seen the place, and I hoped (and still hope) that my unknown friend--the miner who had given Violet an apple—was among the fortunate ones who escaped.

Scenery—Crow Castle

Modern Shepherd

Scenery near Llangollen

Crow Castle (near Llangollen)

Lake District

Lake District near Grassmere

Ludlow Castle

Scene in Wales

CHAPTER FOURTEEN

Hurrying Through Regions of Smoke and Gloom
—Beautiful Cumberland—A Strange Meeting
—Lecture on Art

I HAD no desire to ride through the industrial
districts which lay ahead of me towards the north,
and therefore was left with two alternatives : turn
west from Wrexham and ride into the heart of the
Welsh hills, or load the mare on a truck and
transport her as far as Kendal, and from there
continue my jaunt over the Cumberland mountains, through the Lake District, and from there
up to Scotland.

Riding through the industrial parts of Yorkshire
would have amounted to a senseless stunt, and I
am sure that neither the mare nor I would have
enjoyed it.

After a short mental debate, I came to the conclusion that I had seen a certain amount of Wales,
and that the Lake District and the Scottish border
country would probably be pleasanter to ride
through than Wales.

129

I

Accordingly, I hired a truck, and loaded Violet, who—though it was her first experience in motoring—climbed on quickly when I led the way, showing her a bunch of carrots.

The first jolts gave her a surprise, but when the truck had turned round in the stable-yard, she settled down to eating, apparently not in the least disturbed by the rumbling of the motor.

When all was ready I sat down in front alongside the driver, whereupon we started out.

The mare, who by this time was greatly attached to me, suddenly missed my company. Not realising that I was in front with the driver, she started to neigh so loudly that it was never necessary to use the motor-horn to warn people out of the way.

Drivers of cars, pedestrians and policemen looked on and laughed as we drove past with our equine Tetrazzini, whom I could not see from the driver's seat.

When we left Wrexham the sun was shining brightly, but on nearing Warrington we drove into a regular smoke-screen which even obscured the sun.

Now we were in the midst of gloomy industrial parts, where the very air is impregnated and saturated with choking smells of smoke and fumes.

The dismal rows of low brick houses, and even the grass and scraggy bushes which miraculously grow here and there in this melancholy region, are black with the soot which has settled on them.

The muddy banks of slimy streams and canals are

streaked with layers of oil and chemical substances, and the inky, turbid and sluggish waters emit foul smells, which increase one's feelings of depression and gloom.

When I listened to the mare's neighs, I could not help thinking that she was lucky to be where she was, for the region we sped through is not fit for innocent animals to live in. And to think that men make such infernos to manufacture things which are necessary to create material prosperity : the backbone of modern civilisation.

Many ruins which had once been busy factories were deserted, some being on the point of tumbling down, their rows of broken windows looking sinister —like the hollow eye-sockets of grinning human skulls.

As we drove past long rows of dismal smelly dens, which serve as human habitations, even the thought of living in them made me shudder.

Like phantoms, veritable effigies of men and women stood at some of the doors whilst numerous dirty children played in side streets, laughing and shouting, obviously quite unaffected by their surroundings, which they—luckily, perhaps—have never had the opportunity of comparing with better ones.

Apart from the peculiar dialect which is spoken in these regions, it is not surprising that England's most famous comedians have come from there, for to be a humorist a person must have a keen sense of proportion.

Hardships and suffering bring out and develop this sense where it exists, whereas material and physical prosperity are apt to have the opposite effect.

In essence, humour plays on misfortunes, adversities or human failings. To see them from an amusing angle, and to express them in words which will provoke laughter, a person must have a keen sense of proportion, for anything that is out of proportion excites laughter.

Half-way between Preston and Lancaster the atmosphere gradually became clearer. At first the sun looked like a pale orange disc, but, by degrees, as the smoke became thinner, its rays began to penetrate, until, finally, it again shone down on us in its full glory.

Once more under a blue sky and among green fields, I felt as if we had just come out of a tunnel.

In spite of the fact that I had reassuringly spoken to Violet during a short stop, she still seemed to think that I had deserted her, and therefore she kept up her neighing.

We arrived at Kendal without incident; and when I stepped off the truck to unload the mare, she greeted me with nickerings of joy and affection.

Poor old girl, she had had a long ride—and now was glad to see me.

A kindly policeman offered to help me unload her, but I did not require his assistance, for she stepped off the truck as if she had been used to it all her life.

A little later, when she had her nose in a manger filled with oats, she soon forgot all about her latest experience, and as I walked away I could hear her munch her fodder, every now and again giving a snort of contentment.

Early next morning I went to the stable to prepare Violet for the trek. She had already finished her breakfast when I arrived, so all I had to do was to give her a final brushing down before putting on the saddle.

Whenever I ride I like to do the feeding and grooming of the animal, for to me this is a pleasure : and I am sure that horses appreciate these attentions, which help to befriend them with their riders.

As usual, I went afoot for a while, thus giving the mare a chance to stretch her legs, movements she performed like a cat, at the same time yawning and rolling her eyes.

This, according to the South American *gauchos* (cow-boys), is a sure sign that a horse is well and in good condition. "*Caballo que bosteza, se estira y revuelca, anda lejos,*" they say. This, in English, means : "A horse which yawns, stretches himself and rolls, goes far."

Most of the houses in Kendal are built of grey stone, and some of the steep, narrow alleys with their rough cobblestone steps, are very picturesque.

Following a quiet road which led west, over hills and through two enchanting hamlets, I came to a gate of a villa where I saw several riders who were mounted on elegant hunters.

To my surprise, they greeted me and insisted that I halt for a while to drink a glass of sherry.

My hosts said that they had heard about my arrival in Kendal, and that they had planned to meet me at the outskirts of the town, but as I had started so early we only met as they were setting out.

Whilst I had a stirrup cup, Violet was propitiated with apples and sugar, and soon after the two of us continued our leisurely trip towards Lake Windermere.

Here and there, in hollows, or nestled against the slopes of hills, were farms, and cattle or sheep were grazing in fields.

In these regions, like farther north, fields are separated by stone walls which wind up mountains and twist along hills like gigantic dark grey snakes.

Sometimes, inquisitive horses came galloping towards us, snorting and playfully kicking the air as they raced up and down along the stone walls which were between us and them. When they came to the ends of their fields they would halt, and with raised heads watch us go away, every now and again neighing loudly as if calling to us to return for another game.

Violet thoroughly enjoyed these conversations, which she kept up even long after we were out of earshot.

Jogging over the top of a hill, I suddenly saw Lake Windermere below us.

Its delicate blue showed up to perfection against the dark green of the wooded hills on the opposite side. To give grandeur to this wonderful panorama, rocky mountains towered high into the azure sky, across which drifted a few snow-white clouds, which were reflected on the mirror-like surface of the glittering lake below.

I had been advised to take the ferry across the lake, and then to follow a quiet drive which leads through the woods along its western shore.

Accordingly, I rode down-hill towards the place where I knew was the ferry, and when a few cars were safely parked on the flat boat, I walked on with Violet, who pretended to be nervous when the engine began to throb and puff.

Knowing that she was quite safe, and that she was merely trying to show off, I took no notice of her ; but, instead, chatted with passengers, who envied me for riding on a horse instead of in a car.

In the meantime, two ladies who happened to have some apples, gave them to the mare, who was so interested in their flavour that she quite forgot about the puffing engine.

On *terra firma* once more, I tied her to a rail under a shady tree, whereupon I went into the bar of the Ferry Hotel to have a glass of beer and a couple of sandwiches.

My equine sweetheart, who by this time had

learnt a trick or two, whinnied and pawed the ground until she attracted the barmaid's attention —half the battle towards receiving a few lumps of sugar.

Whilst I was enjoying my simple lunch, a gentleman came to talk to me. In the course of conversation, he asked me if I was " hiking " through, to which question I answered that I was merely riding about to see the country, my immediate destination being any place I happened to come to in the evening.

" What a splendid idea," my new acquaintance exclaimed ; " there's nothing like a horse to see the country properly—— By the way," he continued enthusiastically, " if you want to know something about a *real* ride, I advise you to buy a book I am reading just now. It's all about a fellow who is supposed to have ridden from Buenos Aires to Washington. *Some* ride, if it's true, you know ; not just a leisurely jaunt like yours—— Maybe you know the book. It was written by a man with a devilish name ; a sort of sneeze with T's, CH's, S's and F's all mixed up."

Chuckling inwardly, I answered that I knew something about the book in question, and I agreed that a name such as its author's was devilish, or even worse. Having pointed out the disadvantages of being burdened for life with such a name, I said that I could speak with feeling because I happened to be the unfortunate bearer of the name in question.

When my interlocutor realised that I was not joking, he laughed heartily, and—not very much against my will—made me drink another glass of beer.

As it happened, my new friend is the editor of a well-known newspaper, in which he published a very amusing story about our strange meeting.

Later, I heard that the ferryman had expressed surprise at the way in which I had allowed Violet to do as she liked on his boat, for whilst I chatted with some of the passengers, he had remarked to a bystander : " Well, t'chap 'at belongs ter this 'ere gallowa' doesn't know mich abaht horses."

Perhaps the old Cumberland navigator was right, but I leave Violet to decide this—and she is not likely to tell anyone what she thinks, unless it happens to be about fodder she wants.

It was no easy matter to leave the little group of people who, in the meantime, had assembled near the mare, but finally I succeeded, and soon was alone again, riding at a slow walk along a shady drive which skirts the western bank of Lake Windermere.

Sitting sideways on the saddle, I let the mare go along as she liked whilst I admired the lake and its lovely surroundings.

Coming to an open patch, Violet went to the shore to have a drink, and when I dismounted she immediately started to eat of the luscious grass which grew there, every now and again, for a change, taking a big mouthful of bracken.

" Glorious weather for a canter," a male voice suddenly startled me.

Turning round to find out where it had come from, I saw a bearded face and two eyes which peeped at me from under a wide-brimmed hat which protruded from behind a bush.

" Yes, perfect," I answered, as the owner of the shaggy beard rose to come towards me.

In perfect keeping with his general appearance, the man held a palette and several brushes in one hand—whilst as he came towards me—he offered me a cigarette with the other.

Having accepted it, we conversed for a while, and then the tame-looking " Wild Man from Borneo " asked me if I was interested in art.

Pretending to be even more stupid and crude than I am in reality, I answered that I hardly understand what the word means, whereupon, with a flourish of his palette and brushes, he began to give me a lecture. In order better to explain what he meant by certain statements, he invited me to follow him behind the bush where stood his easel, which supported what this painter must have thought the world would soon acclaim as a master-piece.

As far as I could see, my friend had dabbed numerous spots of lilac, purple, blue, green and pink paint on the canvas, and here and there— probably in spasmodic fits of inspiration—he had boldly smeared a number of thick, dark blue and green lines which, he explained, represented the hills beyond the lake, the multi-coloured and dazzling spots symbolising water movement and certain reflections.

" You see," the genius at my side said, with pride, " I am what we call an ' impressionist '."

Looking straight into the speaker's child-like eyes I nodded as if understanding perfectly, for if I had told him what my impressions were, he would most likely have had a fit—which would have spoilt my day.

" Of course," he went on, with a superior and at the same time compassionate smile, " I quite realise that your untrained eyes do not see as mine do, and, therefore, my painting does not convey to you what it does to me."

Unable to decide whether to shake my head, or if nodding would be the diplomatic thing to do, I turned to stare at the *magnum opus* on the easel, at the same time thinking that Nature was kind in having given me ordinary eyes wherewith to admire her works in my simple and crude way ; not with distortions of colour and shape so many of our modern painters and sculptors affect for the sake of publicity which, alas, is one of the greatest and most lucrative arts of our day.

Far be it from me to pose as a connoisseur in matters of art. As far as I am concerned, I apply the word " art " to anything done, or produced, by the genius of Man ; anything wherewith he earns my admiration, or succeeds in stirring my senses.

True, there is also art in ugliness and in other evils of life, but here I am only considering colour, form, shape and beauty as represented by immortal masters who—by many of our modern dabblers— are accused of being too " photographic " and " realistic " to be " spiritual."

Like cunning card-sharpers, self-styled " modernists," by making use of the mysterious—though weighty—ace-card " SPIRIT," cleverly palm off their wares to the ever-gullible public.

If I pretended, as so many do, to be in raptures over any work of " art," even if so-called experts or people with vested interests acclaimed it as the product of super-genius, I would merely be a *poseur*, a fool and a snob.—And a snob must, perforce, be a combination of the two.

When a person goes out of his or her way to affect the old and " chewed-out " stunt of appearing " arty," and thus hopes to be noticed, this is an admittance of weakness, for filthy unkempt long hair, fancy beards, " Bohemian " attire, and pretended disregard of social customs, modes and manners, no more qualify a person as an artist than the wearing of a morning-coat and top-hat would turn a gorilla into a gentleman.

Little the wiser for the painter's details about the profound mysteries of his art, I whistled to the mare, who immediately pricked up her ears and looked towards me.

Owing to the bush which obstructed her line of vision, she could not see the painting on the easel.

Perhaps this was just as well, for horses are also "impressionists," their reactions to sights they are not familiar with sometimes being violent and even dangerous for people who happen to stand in their line of flight.

Having thanked the artist for his most interesting and instructive lecture, I mounted once more, and, as I turned in the saddle to wave a final farewell, I was just in time to see him go behind the bush to give the finishing dabs to his *chef-d'œuvre*, which, I hope, will bring its progenitor fame and fortune.

CHAPTER FIFTEEN

Grasmere—Into the Heart of the Fells—
England's Native Ponies—Nature's Champagne
—" Yanks " and " Limeys "

ROUGHLY two miles from the northern end of
the lake I came out of the shady woods. At this
point I took a lane which branched off in a north-
westerly direction, winding over hills, through
fields and patches of forest.

Without meeting a single vehicle, I trotted along
happily until I came to the River Brathay, which
I crossed by riding over Skelwith Bridge, from
where I took a quiet road which led towards
Grasmere.

Violet did not like some of the steep inclines, so I
dismounted to go afoot, letting her follow behind me
like a faithful dog.

Tinted blood-red by the evening sun, the scenery
around me was grand to the point of being overpowering.

Below me I saw Lake Grasmere, glittering
like molten metal, and beyond its surrounding

fields of delicate green towered the rocky masses of Rydall Fell, Fairfield, Helvellyn and Helm Crag.

Beyond them, high up in the vermilion sky—like a vast herd of celestial sheep—a mass of wavy golden clouds completed the unforgettable picture which held me spellbound until the mare pushed her head against my back, as if to remind me that she had had a long day, and that it was high time she received her ration of oats.

The shadows of evening were creeping up the mountains when I began my search for a stable, which, for the first time on my ride, I could not find.

A local inhabitant informed me that he knew of a farm, situated on the outskirts of the village, where they might be willing to take care of my mare for the night.

Fortunately my kind informer was right, for the farmer proved to be an excellent person, who knew how to look after a horse.

A finer type of man than this Cumberland farmer I have never seen.

About fifty years of age, tall, square-set and powerful, he was a picture of health and vigour.

His clean-shaven, firm but kindly face was bronzed by the sun, and his greyish-blue eyes had in them a look of independence and yet friendliness. A shock of curly grey hair and a brow furrowed deep by weather and care, would have made this man's head a rare model for a sculptor.

When he told me that his family had farmed in

the district for over four hundred years, I was not surprised, for the man looked as if he were part of the very rocks and soil.

Comparing his rugged figure with the towering mountains near us, I was impressed by an unmistakable resemblance between them, for the man almost appeared to belong to the mineral world, being an animated statue hewn out of local rock.

Shaking his powerful hand felt like making personal contact with the peaks which now glowed in the last flickering rays of the setting sun.

There being no other accommodation available, I was obliged to go to an hotel, where I felt rather out of place in my soiled riding attire.

In the dining-room, some of the guests cast sideways glances at me as if I were a savage, but even the turned-up noses I noticed here and there did not spoil my meal, after which I went to bed to sleep the sleep of the just.—A marvellous day was behind me.

Having risen early—in order to be on my way before the sun became hot—I had breakfast, whereupon I went to the farm to saddle up.

Violet, who was grazing in a field, recognised me from afar. Galloping, goat jumping and neighing, she came tearing towards me, and when I opened the gate she followed me into the farm-yard, where I groomed her whilst chatting with my friend, the farmer.

My plans for the day were made. I would find

Lake District

Skelwick Bridge—Lake District

Lake Windermere

A tarn

Grisedale Creek

Gossip

On the slopes of Helvellyn

Fell ponies

the old pony track which winds up to the high pass between Helvellyn and Fairfield, from there descend to Ullswater, and then go on to Penrith —a stiff journey for a horse unaccustomed to mountaineering.

About a mile north of Grasmere I left the main road, and, passing through a little gate on my right, found myself on the pony track I had been looking for.

Ahead, and across the valley behind me, towered mountains, partly hidden by mists which slowly lifted as the rays of the sun became warmer.

At first the track was fair, winding up-hill alongside a rumbling and foaming mountain stream, but after a while the incline became so steep that the now steaming mare occasionally stopped to recover her breath.

Higher and higher we climbed, and when the path became too steep and rough, I dismounted to go afoot.

In spite of the cool atmosphere, I was soon dripping with perspiration. Every now and again I sat down to rest, and at the same time to admire the glorious scenery around and below me.

During one of these halts I was joined by two hikers, who were on their way up to the peak of Helvellyn.

The track was now so steep and rough that it would have been cruel to make the mare carry me, for she had to use all her strength to carry her own weight up the steep, rocky slopes.

K

Across the narrow valley, on the lower slopes of Fairfield, shepherds were rounding up sheep, whistling to their wonderfully trained dogs, who obeyed the signals in an almost uncanny manner.

Owing to the stillness, we could hear every sound with remarkable clearness.

When members of a herd of half-wild Fell ponies neighed to Violet she became very excited, snorting, stamping and answering their calls of liberty and freedom as if a dormant instinct had suddenly been awakened within her.

Whistling to give them confidence, I slowly approached the ponies, and when I was within a few yards of them I stopped to admire the sturdy animals, whose history—as a distinctive breed—goes back to the reign of Henry VIII.

* * * * *

In those days vast herds of wild ponies roamed through the forests which covered the greater part of Britain.

When these animals invaded the relatively few patches of land under cultivation at the time, it can easily be imagined what havoc they played with the crops.

Encouraged by the King, agriculture was spreading rapidly. Finally, in order to protect the primitive farmers, Henry VIII gave orders to kill the wild ponies, which were a great nuisance.

With the subsequent persecution, and owing to the fact that forests were rapidly being cut down to make arable land, the ponies took refuge in the then wild country to the east of the Pennine Range, in the hills of Wales, Scotland, Westmorland, and Cumberland, in the moorland of Exmoor and Dartmoor, and in the New Forest.

Separated by inhabited regions, the ponies in the different regions—due to natural selection and adaptation to climatic and topographical conditions—began to develop characteristics, which in the course of many generations, formed them into different breeds which, fortunately, survive to this day.

Thus, on the mainland of Britain, we have the following breeds, all descendants of the original British forest pony :

Highland,
Galloway,
Fell,
Dales,
Welsh,
Exmoor,
New Forest,
Dartmoor.

(I purposely omit the Shetland and Connemara ponies).

Adaptation to conditions has made the Dales, Fell, Highland and Welsh ponies into strong weight-carriers, unexcelled for work in their native regions.

Square-chested, standing between 13.2 and 14.2 hands, they are nimble and sure-footed as chamois, amazing walkers, very docile, and generally nice dispositioned animals.

Unlike Hackney, Polo and other artificially bred ponies, who—owing to the thoroughbred blood in their veins—are nervous and excitable, the invaluable characteristics of the pure British pony are docility, hardiness and powerful physique— wonderful qualities which are always weakened through experiments in cross-breeding them with " blooded " ponies which, usually, are just undersized thoroughbreds.

To members of Pony Clubs and young riders in general, I particularly recommend Fell, Welsh and Exmoor ponies, whose endowments make them safe, lovable and generally excellent mounts for young, and even old riders.

*   *   *   *   *

At last, puffing and panting, the two hikers and I reached the highest point of the pass, where we sat down to have a well-earned rest.

The magnificent views we had from this point fully rewarded us for the arduous climb. Whilst the three of us gazed into the distance, Violet sought her own recompense, which she found in the shape of grass which grew between some of the rocks near us.

Within a stone's throw from us, at the foot of the last high wall of rock leading up to the summit of Helvellyn, was a tiny lake, known as Grisedale Tarn.

Our immediate surroundings were so barren and rough that they brought back memories of the highland of Bolivia and Peru.

Having wished my two companions farewell and good luck, I watched them for a while as they resumed the climb towards their goal, and soon after I started the downward journey towards Ullswater, which was not yet in sight.

Recalling unpleasant situations in the desolation of the Andes, I was now glad to think that I was not weeks away from civilisation and a good square meal.

Alone once more, I followed the rough track down Grisedale Creek, jumping over stones and down rocky steps, some of which were so nasty that I had to coax the mare before she followed me.

As she had never been on so rough a trail, I was a little nervous, and took care to pick the easiest steps, for I was afraid she might twist or even break a leg.

Soon, however, we came down to parts where the going was much easier.

Fell ponies are so used to rocks and stones that they can travel at full speed over them, straight up or down steep slopes, picking their way with the agility of mountain goats.

Following a romping stream we wound our way down the creek, shut in on both sides by the high, rocky slopes of Eagle Crag on our left, and St. Sunday Crag on the right.

Looking at some of the stone walls which ran far up and along the mountain-sides, I wondered how long they had stood there, who on earth had built them, and how long the completion of these gigantic tasks had taken.

Down in the lower regions where the forest-land begins, I passed a group of middle-aged holiday-makers who were picnicking near the stream.

" This beats the best champagne," one of them exclaimed, holding up a goblet filled with crystal-clear water.

I hesitated for a moment, wondering if I should tell the merry picnickers that farther up-stream I had seen the decomposed carcass of a sheep lying in the water. However, thinking that my infor-mation might spoil their day, I rode past the merry people without saying a word.

After all, " What the ear does not hear, the heart (and stomach, I hope) does not grieve."

Down and down the path wound, until, coming out of a beautiful wood, I suddenly saw the pale blue lake, Ullswater.

Skirting its shores for roughly eight miles, I came to its northern end, from where I was obliged to follow the motor-road towards Penrith, a distance of about five miles.

" Au revoir, beautiful John Peel country," I felt like shouting as I looked back at the imposing sky-line behind me.

The Sun had already dipped behind the jagged fells, and the birds were beginning to sing their evening songs when I jogged through the southern outskirts of Penrith.

The knowledge that the mare was happy in a horse-box helped to make my evening an enjoyable one.

Sitting in the cosy bar of my little hotel, I chatted with several new acquaintances, at the same time watching other patrons who were throwing rubber rings at a board into which were screwed small hooks, every one of which represented a certain number. In the north this, at first sight easy, but, in fact, very difficult game, is played instead of " darts," which is the favourite pastime in " pubs " in the south.

Among the few tourists who came in for refreshment were several Americans, probably on their way to, or from, Scotland by car.

As on many former occasions, I had the opportunity to observe that the local men eyed the visitors from overseas with disdain, and when the tourists left to resume their journey, I heard half-whispered grunts and remarks which were far from complimentary.

The mutual dislike which exists between the present-day Englishman and American is incomprehensible to me, and I am at a loss to understand what could have caused it to have taken root to such an extent that it has become an obsession with many people on both sides of the Atlantic Ocean.

Judging by my own observations, I venture to state that, on the whole, Englishmen dislike Americans more than their cousins do the English.

To me the ridiculous part of it all is that the vast majority of rabid " Yank " or " Limey " haters have never been beyond their respective borders. They merely slander one another because they seem to think it is the right thing to do.

Probably the origin of this mutual dislike can be traced back to the American War of Independence, which, though practically forgotten to-day, has, nevertheless, left this nasty " hang-over."

The harbouring and inventing of grievances, like jealousy and hatred, are painful mental afflictions from which, particularly, weak-minded persons are apt to suffer. Since the vast majority of human beings have weak minds—or no minds of their own at all—it is not surprising that they brood over matters which are non-existent, or do not affect them in the least.

The teaching of twisted historical facts, and the majority of men's inability to think for themselves, favour bigotry and blind nationalism which the masses mistake for patriotism.

Among themselves, English people are extremely tolerant and fair-minded, but, being insular, they are apt to think that all other but British customs, ways and manners must be wrong.

In America I have been asked countless times whether I am a Protestant or a Catholic, a question I have never yet had to answer in England, where religious opinions are rightly considered to be strictly private.

Jews, though superficially accepted as equals, find it difficult to mix in society, unless they happen to possess the necessary material assets to buy the doubtful privileges.

" I don't mind Jews, but I don't like them," is the attitude of most Englishmen, who look upon Hebrews as a race apart, and therefore prefer not to mix with them.

CHAPTER SIXTEEN

Across the Scottish Border—Gretna Green—
Behind a Counter the Village Smithy Stands—
" If You Have Heard this One about the
Scotchman, Stop Me "

ABOUT half a mile out of Penrith I left the busy
Great North Road, and, by making a small detour,
kept away from traffic until I reached Carlisle,
where, after the mare had been re-shod, I left her
in an excellent stable.

Friends who had heard about my arrival insisted
on driving me to their home, where, after dinner
we chatted until our eyelids began to droop.

Next morning, for the first time since I had
started my ride, the sky looked dismal and gloomy,
and shortly after I had left Carlisle, occasional
showers began to fall.

Near Gretna Green, two painted metal disks
mark the English-Scottish border.

When Violet had stepped across this otherwise
invisible division I came to the first of the two

famous "Smithy Shops," the "House of Ten Thousand Marriages," as it is sometimes called.

Having dismounted to inspect the place, I found the doors locked and the wooden window-shutters closed. The white-washed walls and the general atmosphere about the house suggested rather a morgue than a place where "stunt" marriages are performed on a large scale.

Over one of the window-shutters was stuck a large poster announcing that the establishment was for sale by auction.

Perhaps the acute economic depression from which the world was suffering at the time had even affected the marriage business, which has put Gretna Green in the head-lines of some sensational newspapers ; or, maybe, the excellent gentleman who used to tie the nuptial knots over the anvil, has amassed sufficient "scrap-iron" to be able to retire in peace, leaving the pairs of firmly-welded members of his long matrimonial chain-gang to fight out their own battles.

Riding away from the place, I noticed a lantern above the door, and I wondered if its clear glass had ever blushed red when couples passed under it before going through a ceremony which would even cause laughter among primitive dwellers in the wildest parts of our strange world.

Half a mile farther along the main road I came to the village, Gretna Green, where a patrolman of the Automobile Association greeted Violet with a juicy apple.

From this man I learnt that the other " Marriage House " was farther along the road, in the centre of the small village, near the church.

Trotting round a bend I could not possibly have missed the place, which is plastered with big advertisements, rivalling the most conspicuous I have ever seen in " Two-Penny Shows " at fairs.

As I approached, a few tourists stared at me with surprise, perhaps wondering if I was a paid " dummy," riding about to give the village an " atmosphere."

Having searched for a while, I found a place where I tied the mare, for I wanted to see the interior of the " Blacksmith's Shop," and I had made up my mind to have a little game with the " smithy," who only knows how to " nail " couples together, and who probably thinks that horseshoes are merely lucky charms.

Passing through a door, I entered a room which had the appearance of a curio shop and booking-office combined into one.

On one side was a counter behind which stood a corpulent woman, who wore an electric-blue gown, made of what appeared to be silk.

" Good morning," I said, " I wonder if the blacksmith has time to shoe my horse ? "

Had the place been a bank, and the person behind the counter a cashier, my words could not have sounded more incongruous if I had said I had brought a steam-shovel I would like the bank to mend for me.

Seeing the look of surprise and bewilderment on the woman's face, I had to make great efforts to suppress a chuckle which tickled my throat like the rising gases of soda-water.

" I'm afraid . . . ahem . . . we don't shoe . . . ahem . . . horses here," the woman stuttered when she had recovered from the first shock ; " but if you go farther up the road, you will find a good . . . ahem . . . blacksmith, who will do the job for you."

Pretending to be puzzled and annoyed, I asked what on earth the sign above her door might mean, for, unless my eyes deceived me, on it was written, in large letters, that this was a blacksmith's shop.

To this the embarrassed woman answered that the place had originally, many years ago, been a forge, but that nowadays it was used to marry people in.

Trying hard to look innocent and mystified, I pushed back my hat and scratched my head, but before I had time to ask another stupid question, the business instinct got the better of the woman, who told me that if I wanted to see the " marriage room " this would cost me sixpence.

Having paid my admission fee, I was allowed to pass through a crude turnstile which leads into the " blacksmith's shop "—*i.e.*, the " marriage room."

Were it not for a dummy furnace, bellows and two or three painted anvils of different sizes, the room and its general atmosphere might easily be taken for a village slaughter-house in recess.

A couple of hammers and tongs, the handles of which betray the fact that they have never been used, a few rusty horseshoes, and a handful of coal—now grey with dust which has settled on them during the years they must have done duty as make-believe on the hearth—complete what is supposed to look like a blacksmith's shop which, incidentally, has no other doors than two narrow turnstiles which serve as " way in " and " way out " respectively.

As I looked around the " forge " I remembered an epitaph I had seen on an old tombstone in Hampshire, and I slowly muttered the words :

> " My Sledge and Hammer lie reclined
> My Bellows too have lost their Wind
> My Fire is out, and Forge decay'd
> And in the Dust my Vice is laid."

Having passed through the turnstile marked " way out," I once more found myself in the ante-room where the stout woman behind the counter unsuccessfully tried to make me buy a souvenir.

More tourists were arriving when I stepped out of the famous " forge," which would make a perfect counter-match if it were " transplanted " alongside the divorce court building of Reno in the United States of America .

When one imagines the tidal-wave of visitors the Gretna Green " Smithy's Shop " would attract to Reno, one comes to the conclusion that the Chamber of Commerce of that city lacks vision, initiative and enterprise.

A little publicity, " ballyhoo " and, perhaps, wayside posters, would immediately start a regular tidal-wave of tourists, for true American citizens could not resist the call of :

VISIT RENO
AND SEE
YE OLDE SCOTTISH BLACKSMITH'S
SHOPPE
AND
THE WORLD-FAMOUS DIVORCE MILL
WITH
ITS LIGHTNING NULLITY-DECREE
DIPLOMA PRESS.
BE MODERN : MARRY AND DIVORCE
WITHIN 24 HOURS
TWO BANQUETS IN ONE DAY !

Thinking that I was wasting my time and talents in riding about like a Don Quixote when such, and similar important human problems called for solution, I approached Violet, who was now surrounded by a few local loafers.

Wondering what the leather buttons on my Argentine bridle were for, somebody had undone one, the result being that the bit had fallen out of the mare's mouth.

When I arrived on the scene, one of the local horse experts made efforts to push the bit into the mare's mouth, but as he tried to make her " take " it upside-down, she naturally refused.

Whilst re-adjusting the leather buttons, and putting the bit back in its place, I delivered a lecture for the benefit of the impudent meddlers who were visibly impressed by my flow of language which, as I have mentioned in a preceding chapter, had been vastly improved during my short but profitable stay in Oxford.

Before I had finished my discourse on manners, heredity and pedigree, all the members of my audience, but one, had " faded away," so I finished my speech by asking the only remaining listener to hold the mare whilst I took a photograph.

Having thanked my admirer for his assistance, I resumed my journey towards Annan.

Threatening black clouds were rolling past overhead, driven along by violent gusts of a cold wind. Occasionally, when the sun managed to break through a gap between the clouds, its brilliant beams, like gigantic rays of celestial searchlights, swept over the hilly country and over the waters of the Solway Firth.

The weather was so unpleasant that I took the shortest route towards Annan, riding on the grassy edge of the main road which led through pretty agricultural country, and past a number of neat, homely-looking farm-houses.

Despite previous visits I had made to Scotland, I knew but little about its people, for I never had the opportunity of mixing with the labouring classes or

Fell ponies

Fell stallion

"Violet" in the Fells

farmers until I rode through the southern parts of this interesting country.

Of course, I had heard countless humorous yarns and stories about Aberdeen and its inhabitants ; but hearing is one thing, and seeing is another.

In most countries I have visited there is a region, state or province which is supposed to give birth to the meanest and stingiest people imagination can conceive.

In Italy, to quote only one example, the Genoese have, since time immemorial, been the target of jokes, many of which have been translated into English to be applied to the apocryphal Scotchman who is supposed to be mean enough to snatch a worm from a blind hen, if he needs bait for fishing.

There are people who suspect Scotch wiliness to such an extent that they believe in the existence of a special office in Aberdeen, where many of these stories are supposed to be invented, and sold to amuse the stupid outer-world.

Speaking from personal experience, I have found Scotch people, next to Spaniards, to be the most generous and liberal spenders, whereas, on the other hand, Frenchmen—though they make genial companions and good friends—I have invariably found to have " hard triggers " on their purses.

Scotchmen, perhaps, are *careful* with their money, for the vast majority learn to realise its value in their early childhood.

The land of their birth is rugged and poor, and,

L

therefore, the struggle for existence is a hard one.

Like the Swiss, with whom they have a great deal in common, Scots have migrated to every corner of the world, where many of these hardy pioneers have done great things.

Were it not for vigour, initiative and thoroughness which are national characteristics of the Scots, the country would hardly figure on the map, and many chapters of glorious British history would never have been written, had not Scotland provided England with some great soldiers, statesmen and scholars who have contributed towards the building of the world's biggest empire.

A by no means unique example of Scottish life was brought to my notice during my ride, when I heard about an old farmer whose three sons have risen to be ; one a professor attached to a famous American university, the second a judge, and the third a civil engineer in one of the British colonies.

When a Scotchman is crude, he is, on the other hand, as primitive, uncouth and unimaginative a being as can be found anywhere in the world.

CHAPTER SEVENTEEN

*The Scottish Border Country—Rain and More
Rain—On Superstitions—A Frugal Meal*

HAD it not been for adverse weather conditions,
my ride through the Scottish Border Country
would have been much more enjoyable, for
wherever I went or stayed, I was shown hospitality and kindness, which, at times, was almost
embarrassing.

On several occasions—contrary to the essence
of " Scotch yarns "—people flatly refused to take
money I offered them for food, stabling and fodder :
gestures nobody ever made to me during my journey
through England.

Scots may be slow at making friends, but once
friendships have been made they are of a sincere,
solid and lasting nature.

When I left Dumfries, the sky was grey, and
strong winds were blowing over the hills. I had
not gone far when the heavenly taps opened, and
a cold rain began to pelt down on us with such force

that the mare stopped and put her head between her fore-legs.

Owing to the strong wind, my rain-coat was of little use, and soon water began to trickle down my neck, and my legs—and even the saddle— were soaking wet.

For some strange reason I am unable to explain, I am always happy when I am out in the rain. On such occasions, although nature has not gifted me with a good voice, I usually try to sing like a Caruso, for, when I need not bother about my clothes, I love a good downpour and the noise of a storm.

Luckily (for me and my fellow-men) I only sing when I am alone, and out in the open, for if I exercised my vocal cords indoors, the chances are that—voluntarily or otherwise—I would soon find myself outside, where my voice harmonises well with the noises made by the furious elements.

Heading into the strong wind and driving rain did not please the mare, who moved with reluctance, every now and again shaking her head when water was blown into her ears, which she carried flattened back like a vicious mule about to kick.

The change of temperature was so sudden that I began to shiver. By degrees my fingers became so stiff and numbed that I could hardly hold the reins, and the periodical re-adjusting of the saddle and girth became a task the difficulties of which can be compared with the playing of a one-man band by a man wearing boxing-gloves.

Here and there, where fir trees grew, their fragrant scent, mixed with the rich smell of wet earth, made me inhale deeply.

The whistling and whining of the wind through telephone wires, trees and hedges, the drumming of the mare's hoofs, and the splashing of rain, were the only noises I could hear when I interrupted my song.

Every now and again I saw miserable-looking birds who were hiding in the shelter of trees and bushes, their drawn-in heads and bristling wet feathers making them look like tiny hedgehogs.

A weasel which had probably been flooded out of its hole, came out of a bush, for all the world like a peculiar bounding snake.

Paying no attention to my calls and to the clattering of hoofs immediately behind it, the weasel ran along the road for some time before making for the hedge, from where it watched us pass with curiosity and what appeared to be defiance.

The twenty-six miles we covered that day must have seemed like fifty to the mare.

Arriving at Sanquhar I had some difficulty in finding a stable, but finally a cartman offered me an empty stall and all the fodder and bedding a horse could wish for.

Poor Scottish villages, with their small square stone houses, are not attractive to the eye. When it rains, as it did when I arrived in Sanquhar, such places are very dismal, but, fortunately, the interiors of the houses are warm, clean and cosy ; qualities I greatly appreciated that evening.

The " wee " inn where I found quarters was delightful, and the kindly people who ran it did everything they could to make me feel comfortable and at home.

Whilst an attractive Scotch lassie cooked an excellent meal for me, I was invited to sit near the kitchen stove to dry my clothes.

The weather had turned so cold, and I was so wet, that I had not to be asked twice.

Later in the evening, local farmers joined me in the kitchen, where we sat on benches and wooden chairs, which were placed in a semi-circle in front of the stove.

The older members of this genial and friendly assembly discussed the " good old days " when the stage-coaches were the means of transportation, emphasising their occasional curses at motor traffic by puffing out smoke like volcanoes in eruption.

One of the group gradually monopolised the word, telling his listeners stories about the old coaching days.

There was no need for him to tell me that he had once been an ostler, for he looked as if he had walked out of a Dickens novel.

The white hair on his semi-bald head was getting very thin, and out of his round face peeped two blue eyes, the wrinkles and pouches below which changed as he accentuated his words or smiled. Whenever he came to the end of an amusing yarn he joined in the laughter, holding his bulging mid-section with both hands, as if afraid that it would fall out from under the chequered waistcoat on which was the shine of many years, especially where a heavy watch-chain rubbed against it.

Influenced by strong blasts of wind which occasionally snorted down the chimney, and by the incessant noise of rain falling outside, the conversation gradually veered to spooky subjects, and soon I heard one ghost and mystery story after another, some of them being so creepy that they would have given impressionable ladies permanent waves.

Considering the relatively good education people in England, Wales and Scotland enjoy, it is surprising how superstitious the vast majority of them are.

Not only in rural districts, but even in cities, and among so-called intelligent people, I have frequently met persons who, though they profess to be members of the Christian Church, firmly believe in hoodoo, sorcery and black magic.

Quack doctors, fortune tellers, clairvoyants, un-qualified sellers of patent medicines and many other dangerous sharks, exploit these weaknesses of their victims, who willingly part with their money to be given " consultations " and " treatment."

I know a number of people, considered to be highly educated, who regularly visit their " spiritual doctors," whose advice they seek and follow, in social and even in financial matters.

The different churches to which these people flock every Sunday, seem merely to be places for social gatherings, for although the " faithful " in question believe that they are the children of an omnipotent God, their faith in Him is so weak that they prefer the guidance and protection of lucky charms, colours, numbers, or of some cunning charlatan whose words outweigh any that come from the lectern or pulpit.

If I tried to put down on paper the many popular superstitions which have come to my notice, I am afraid they would fill several chapters.

Although some people are fond of pretending that they do not take omens of good or bad luck seriously, they are, nevertheless, afraid of certain superstitions, such as sitting thirteen persons at the same table, looking at a new moon through glass, or passing under a ladder, even if nobody happens to be on it to drop paint or a tool on passers below.

Incredible as it may seem, it is, nevertheless, a fact, that even to-day there are many people—especially in English country districts—who still believe in witchcraft.

A scholarly clergyman told me about a number of cases which border on the incredible.

To cite only one staggering example of the abysmal ignorance which goes hand in hand with superstition, I must take the reader to a village near the Welsh border, where an old woman practises quackery tricks which rival even those of African witch doctors.

Among her " cures " she has one for the whooping cough. To perform this miracle she catches a mouse, and when it has been skinned, the patient must eat it raw !

During my travels through Britain I have heard about so many haunted houses and ghosts that I have lost count of them.

If, at a dinner party, there is a lull in the conversation, somebody has only to start talking about " psychic " matters to have everybody listening or conversing, for few are the persons in Britain who are not interested in this subject.

* * * * *

When I left Sanquhar, the weather was still wet and dreary, but later in the day the sun occasionally broke through the heavy clouds.

Unfortunately, I was obliged to follow the main road towards Kilmarnock, but as there was little traffic, the day's ride was quite enjoyable.

For a long stretch the winding road led along the River Nith, which, here and there, was visible, deep down below, through gaps in the trees.

Towards evening it again began to rain heavily, and I was glad when the mare was in a good stable, where she enjoyed the reward for the thirty-three miles she had carried me that day.

In the evening, friends who had heard about my arrival, joined me in the little hotel where I stayed, and until late we " chewed the rag," talking about every imaginable subject—even though we knew little about most of them.

My friends, being Scotch to the marrow, and true to type, did their utmost to convince me that their native land ranks first in everything in the world.

Until I was beginning to doze in my chair, I was fairly bombarded with evidence of Scotland's supreme greatness, and when I was finally allowed to fold up my wings for the night, I almost believed that Burns is the greatest of great poets, that Scottish doctors and scientists have saved the human race, and that England would still be in a state of barbarism, were it not for Scotland supplying her with statesmen, archbishops, soldiers, engineers, artists, fish, meat, vegetables, fruit, tweed, etc., etc., all of which, of course, are the best in the " worrld," of which my good friends had seen, and obviously knew, but little.

Dreaming about liberty, freedom and Utopia, I slept soundly until morning, my ecstasy occasionally disturbed by shouts of *liberté, liberta, Freiheit, libertad* and their equivalent in other " uncivilised " tongues, and I had visions of faces which were distorted with blind patriotism, bigotry and fanaticism, as they shouted the words which are to be found in national anthems all over the world—but in reality nowhere else.

No doubt, national pride, like family tradition, is desirable and good when indulged in with moderation and, above all, tact, for both give self-respect and a certain dignity ; but, like excessive religious fervour, these mental attitudes often lead to ridicule, and are dangerous eggs from which strife and wars are hatched ; disasters which could never happen if " civilised " man were the thinker he prides himself to be.

Following an old rough road, I slowly rode towards Paisley. All day long it rained in torrents, and, to make the journey even worse, typical Scotch mists crept over the hills, making visibility very poor.

The road led over hills and past a few small settlements and farms. At noon, coming to a miserable stone house, I was delighted to see a crude board outside it, announcing that refreshments were to be obtained there.

Two goats—who must have heard me approach —came out of the door to have a look at me, presently to be followed by a very stout woman, who had as strong an odour about her as had her two horned and bearded pets.

Speaking with a broad Scotch accent which one could have hewn into grind-stones, she politely asked me what I wanted.

The only refreshments to be had in the place were tea, eggs, milk, bread and cheese—not to mention the overpowering smell of goats.

However, as I was wet, and the mare had found a patch of good grass, I decided to be brave and enter the house.

Like a pearl-diver about to leap into the water, I filled my lungs, and then followed the fat waddling woman, who led the way through a crude kitchen into a bed-sitting-room, where the first breath I took nearly asphyxiated me.

Whilst the two goats were nosing about like dogs, the good woman put a kettle on the fire. Then to my consternation, she collected bread, cheese, butter, knives, sugar, forks and spoons, which she kept in drawers and cupboards, which were filled with none-too-clean looking garments and other odds and ends.

When, at last, everything was ready, I made heroic efforts to swallow the food, all of which, including the tea, had a rank taste of goat.

Whenever I had a chance to do it unobserved, I quickly slipped a piece of cheese or bread into one of my pockets, and when my plate was empty I tackled the tea which, unfortunately, I could not dispose of in any other manner than by forcing it down my throat.

All the time the woman—who was a widow— told me about her sons, who were scattered all over the world, one being in the Mounted Police Force in Canada, another in the Royal Navy, whilst two others had settled down in Australia as sheep farmers.

In an alcove there was a huge " four-poster " bed with heavy curtains which were greasy and full of goats' hair ; and, if my vulgar suspicions were correct, full of insects, the very thought of which made me itch all over.

As soon as I had emptied my cup of tea, I rose to

go outside, my excuse being the safety of the mare.

Obviously delighted with my company, the woman and her two smelly pets followed me, and as soon as I had paid for my meal I rode out into the thick mists, where I emptied my bulging pockets, scattering about bread and cheese, thankful to be breathing the cool moist air once more.

CHAPTER EIGHTEEN

Paisley—An Example of Scottish Hospitality—
A Meeting—Modern Roads and Horse Traffic—
A Display of " Equitación "—An Adventurous
Railway Journey—Back to the Home Stall—
A Dios !

A FEW miles out of Paisley the quiet road I had been following joined the main artery, but luckily I arrived on a Saturday afternoon, and consequently there was but little traffic.

Friends had told me about a big hunting stable I would find in the town, so when I reached the outskirts I asked a policeman, who gave me instructions how to get to them.

As on former occasions—especially in Scotland—the owner of the stables, and the grooms, received me and the mare with great kindness. When the animal was happily installed in a roomy loose-box, I went to a telephone to advise friends that I would arrive at Erskine Ferry, on the southern bank of the River Clyde, at 11 a.m. next day.

Waking up in the morning, I was glad to see that

the sun was shining once more, as if to give me a treat on the last day of my ride.

Whilst I fixed the saddle and kit on the mare, a feeling of sadness came over me, and I wondered when—or if ever—I would again have the opportunity of using these articles, the smell and feel of which always brought back to my mind many happy memories.

Although I was, in a way, pleased to think that I had nearly reached my destination, I was on the other hand, sorry that my ride was to come to an end.

The owner of the stables had not arrived when I was ready to set out, so I paid a groom for the fodder and stabling, whereupon I departed.

Shortly after I had left the last houses of the outskirts of Paisley behind me, I was overtaken by a car, which stopped when it was a few yards ahead of me.

To my surprise, the owner of the stables in which the mare had spent the night, stepped out of the car, and, after having greeted me, insisted on my taking back the money I had given to the groom for stabling and fodder.

Despite the fact that I could give many other examples of Scotch hospitality and generosity, I only mention this one as typical of a number of others I could give.

At the appointed time, I merrily trotted downhill towards Erskine Ferry, and on rounding a shaded curve I saw the River Clyde, on the near banks of which stood a group of people who turned to look in my direction.

One figure—anybody who has ever seen would recognise in a crowd of thousands—raised an arm to greet me from afar, like a friendly Red Indian chief of old.

Of course, this was my friend, " Don Roberto " —Cunninghame Graham, as he is known to the literary world.

Surely, in the " wild and woolly " days, when he had wandered and lived among the Pampas and Red Indians, he had often made this sign of friendly greeting. Now, as I trotted towards him, sitting on one of his old pet-saddles, and using the raw-hide bridles he had given to me, I felt proud to be greeted by the almost mystical figure of " The Last of the Cavaliers," as he is often—and rightly—called.

Scotland has produced many great and remarkable men, high among the most extraordinary of which, no doubt, ranks Cunninghame Graham, whose name—though it is not known to the world-at-large—is destined to grow bigger, and more and more famous with the passing of time.

No sooner had I jumped out of the saddle to greet my friends than Violet lowered her head to graze. Whilst she sampled the grass which grew in different patches, we waited for the ferry to bring over one or two friends. When they arrived, and photographs had been taken, we boarded the flat craft, the mare following me with the indifference of an old " salt " going on his lugger.

Gretna Green

Scottish cottages

Highland bull

Even when a large ocean liner glided past, quite near us, she only casually turned her head, for she was far more interested in the sugar Mr. Cunninghame Graham had thoughtfully brought for her.

Shortly after having landed, my friends departed in their cars, whereupon I trotted parallel with the river, down towards Cardross, near which place was my final goal, " Ardoch," " Don Roberto's " beautiful estate.

Fortunately, the road was made of " Trinidad " (a special kind of asphalt, I believe) which makes an excellent surface for horses to travel over.

Here I must remark that if road engineers took the trouble to study the question carefully, a great deal of unnecessary animal suffering could be avoided if roads were built of suitable materials.

Thousands of horses are still hauling loads over roads throughout England. Since most of the pavement is very hard and slippery, the unfortunate animals' tasks have not only been made extremely difficult, but also a veritable torture.

Whenever I see equine slaves make valiant efforts to get a safe grip on roads, it makes me hold my breath and clench my fists.

Unfortunately, to-day only few people understand enough about horses to enable them to realise that something should be done to minimise the suffering caused by slippery roads.

As I jogged through Dumbarton, people came out of " kirk," looking at so strange an apparition

M

as a man on horse-back (on the day of the " guid "
Lord, too !) with wondering eyes.

Some two miles out of the town, at the foot of an
incline, I sighted the moss-covered stone walls and
the stately trees of " Ardoch," close by the banks
of the Clyde.

Passing through the main gate, I followed a
gravel drive which, flanked by trees, ornamental
bushes and lovely flower-beds, leads to the front
entrance of the neat little house in which a number
of Cunninghame Graham's immortal books were
written.

" Don Roberto " and another friend were waiting
for me, and as soon as I had dismounted the former
took my place in the saddle, mounting (in spite of
his eighty-odd years) with the ease and agility of a
gaucho.

Sitting erect, and skilfully guiding the mare with
the lightest of light touches on the neck and mouth,
he made her go up and down a few times, twisting
and turning her round as if his thoughts were
transmitted to the animal's brain through the bridles
which hung half slack, resting on the first finger of
the rider's left hand.

As I watched man and beast go through a few
evolutions, I had visions of a cavalier preparing to
go into an arena for a joust.

If the usually passive mare had realised that she
was carrying the author of the famous book *The
Horses Of The Conquest*, she could not have reacted
more befittingly, for she arched her neck, pricked

up her ears, and, with rolling eyes and dilated
nostrils, obeyed commands which would have been
imperceptible to the eye of an inexpert observer.

* * * * *

After a delightful stay which lasted a few days,
Violet must have been sorry when I took her out
of the adjoining farm, which is part of my friend's
estate, for whilst she had been there she was allowed
to graze in a field all day, and towards evening she
was taken into a loose-box, where she was given
the best fodder a horse could wish for.

Although my ride had come to an end, there was
yet an experience in store for me, for I had made
up my mind to accompany the mare on her railway
journey to Salisbury, my plan being to travel with
her in the horse-box.

My kind and thoughtful host had omitted no
detail to make our journey a comfortable one, for
when I arrived at the station in Cardross, I found
a sack filled with hay, oats and bran, and, for my
comfort, a treasured blanket " Don Roberto " had
used—many years before—on his travels through
Texas and Mexico, in the days when these parts
of the world were still made unsafe by bands of
marauding Indians, and even more dangerous
white " road agents."

In a parcel I found some food, and two bottles
of beer, which I greatly appreciated during the
journey.

Assisted by the kindly station-master and an obliging porter, the loading of the animal was carried out without a hitch ; and soon after I was installed in the private compartment reserved for grooms.

Being its only occupant, I had visions of a pleasant journey, but I soon found out that this was not to be the case.

After a few bumps the horse-box was safely shunted on to the tail-end of the next passenger train to halt at the station, and when farewells had been exchanged we slowly rolled out of Cardross.

Passing " Ardoch " I waved a final " A Dios " to the servants who had assembled in front of the house to see me pass, and then I patted the mare's head, which peeped out of an opening which connected my compartment with hers.

At first she was afraid and nervous with all the rattling and noise, but soon she found out that no harm was to befall her, whereupon she began to nibble at the sweet-smelling hay I had placed in her manger.

In Glasgow I was shunted on to another train which took us to Edinburgh, where, once more, we had to go through seemingly interminable shunting operations before we were hooked on to an express train going " South."

It was dark when we rattled out of Edinburgh.

As the oil-lamp—which was fixed into the ceiling from outside, through a round aperture in the roof of the carriage—gave insufficient light for reading,

I passed away time by eating, and later lay down on the long seat, ready to sleep. But, alas for the frailty of human hopes !

As the train picked up speed, the springless horse-box jumped, clattered and rattled so much that I feared it would derail at any moment.

The noise was so shocking that the mare stopped eating to look at me with terrified eyes.

Off and on, when I felt so drowsy that I could no longer look out of the window to watch occasional lights flash past, I tried to sleep, only to be shaken up and tossed about with such violence that I thought my ribs would be twisted into knots.

Sleep being out of the question, I then tried to read the large print of advertisements in newspapers I had bought, but in the meantime the oil-lamp had sprung a leak, and the glass bowl under it was gradually filling as the drops fell into it.

Wondering if the beastly thing would finally catch fire, and what I would do in such an event, I sat watching the drops fall, one by one.

Dozing for a few minutes, suddenly to be awakened when I thought I was about to hit the roof, I passed an agonising night in complete darkness, for long before the first streaks of greenish-purple in the sky announced the rising of the sun, to my relief the oil-lamp had given its last dying flicker.

Daylight appeared before the train pulled up in London, where—although I longed for a cup of tea—I could not leave my compartment, being shunted about until I thought demons were playing shuttlecock with my horse-box. The thought that I was so near and yet so far from what I wanted so badly was tantalizing, and it filled me with envy when I guessed that by this time the passengers who had passed a comfortable night in sleeping cars in the front section of the train, must be in taxies speeding through the streets of London.

After a while—by an engine all to ourselves— we were shunted through tunnels beneath London, finally to come out in the neighbourhood of Waterloo Station, where a passing goods train picked us up like a marooned raft in a sea of rails.

I was just beginning to feel more cheerful when we were cast off outside a country station, where not even officials could tell me what was to happen to us. After a wait of some two hours I began to have visions of starving to death in the horse-box, when a porter came to inform me that we were to be picked up by the next train to stop at the deserted station.

After some more shunting, I felt greatly relieved when we were hooked on to an express train, soon once more to be clattered and bounced towards the south.

Being wagged about like the tail of an infuriated rattle-snake, we finally arrived at Salisbury where, after another game of shuttlecock, the horse-box was shunted to a standstill in a siding. When I stepped out of my prison, I tottered and my knees sagged as if I had just come off the most wicked buck-jumper ever to have eaten grass.

The mare looked very happy when she stood on solid ground once more, and as I led her through the town to give her a chance to loosen her limbs before I mounted, she every now and again snorted, as if to say, " Thank goodness that's over ! "

Well outside Salisbury I readjusted the saddle, and then slowly jogged towards Violet's home, which was still some nine miles away.

The foliage of most trees had already assumed beautiful autumn tints, and, high up in the sky—like a swiftly-passing cloud—flew thousands of migrating birds, on their long way to warmer climes.

We had not gone far when it became obvious that the mare recognised the country, for she hurried her steps, sniffed the air, and frequently looked in the direction where she knew was her stable.

When I trotted through one of the gates which lead into the park surrounding " Newhouse," I could hardly believe it that I had been away for forty-three days, for I felt as if I had only set out on my ride a day or two before.

As we had not entered into the park through the main gate, nobody saw us approach the house, but as soon as the drumming of hoofs announced our arrival, the groom came hurrying out of the saddle-room and greeted us with a happy smile.

Even the most casual observer would have noticed how pleased the man was to see his old pet, for, whilst he fondled the mare's head, he beamed like a loving uncle on seeing his favourite niece after a long absence.

In the meantime, obviously someone had advised people in the house that the wanderers had returned for soon Miss M., accompanied by other ladies, came to greet us.

On seeing her mistress, the mare's nostrils dilated and quivered, as she softly nickered her affectionate greetings.

I felt proud when everybody remarked how well and fit the animal looked, for, like most normal human beings, praise (especially when I think it is merited) acts like an agreeable intoxicant on me.

Having taken the saddle off the mare, the groom slyly passed a critical hand over her back, in order to see if there were any signs of saddle-pressure, and when he was satisfied that nothing was wrong, he led her into the loose-box where he had already prepared a soft bed of dry bracken.

After a welcome meal which my thoughtful friend kindly offered to me, I returned to the stable to have a final chat with Violet, whom I found busy munching a liberal ration of oats and bran.

As if to warn me that it was high time to depart if I wanted to catch my train back to London, the exhaust of Miss M.'s car was already snorting outside when I patted the mare's sturdy neck for the last time.

Had she been able to understand my words, I would have whispered to her, " Thank you, old girl, for having shown me your lovely country. I've had a perfect holiday, and I hope you've enjoyed it as much as I did. A Dios, Violet. I hope we meet again, soon."

AFTERWORD

BESIDES many pleasant recollections, my ride through England has given me an idea I will try briefly to put down on paper, hoping that enthusiastic and qualified people will take it up, and work it into something practical, which, I have no doubt, would greatly help to revive long-distance riding, and would bring this healthy and delightful sport within the reach of many who, to-day, are not in a position to afford it. Incidentally, it would—to a certain extent—help trade, and bring back something of the old England we all like to remember, or read about.

If horsemen and members of Pony Clubs all over Great Britain put their heads together, and made rough maps, marking bridle paths and tracks which exist in their respective neighbourhoods, these rough sketches could later be compiled and made into a general map.

English farmers are good " sports," and I have no doubt that few, if any, would object to riders using paths which lead through their fields.

Most riders, I presume, respect private property, and would take care not to leave gates open, nor would they litter fields with paper, tins and empty bottles, as hikers, motorists and picnickers often do.

Innkeepers and farmers could be consulted to find out if they have, or could make, accommodation for stabling horses.

During my ride I stopped in a number of inns where empty stables and stalls were waiting to be used, and several innkeepers expressed their hope that my unexpected arrival with a horse would prove to be the forerunner of visits by other riders.

If all such details as inns and other halting places, bridle-paths and lanes were compiled at the headquarters of an Equestrian Touring Club, small signposts could later be put up to guide riders through gates and fields which, otherwise, would be difficult to find.

If enthusiasts did this in their respective regions, the cost would be insignificant.

Finally, simple maps could be produced (perhaps in the shape of booklets), indicating bridle-paths and places where riders and their mounts could spend the nights.

Whenever I mentioned this idea to innkeepers, they were most enthusiastic about it, and expressed their willingness to clean out their now disused stables and stalls, and to stock fodder and bedding.

A riding holiday is healthier—for the body as well as for the mind—than a stay at a crowded seaside resort. Even if a horse has to be hired, the cost is not prohibitive if fodder and stabling can be obtained at reasonable prices.

To see England properly, I recommend viewing

it from the saddle, for the smell and creaking of leather, and the company of a horse give it an atmosphere imaginative people can to-day only find in old novels.

If these crudely and briefly put ideas of mine appeal to horsemen who happen to have time and leisure to sit down and work them out into something practical, I leave it to them to get together and start an organisation which, I feel convinced, would have enormous possibilities ; not only to give people pleasure, but also to help revive one of the finest sports the lovely English countryside offers to any healthy man, woman and even child.

Should able and practical people make use of my suggestion, and work these suggestions into something alive, I would, indeed, be pleased to think that my leisurely jaunt has not been made in vain, as far as my fellow men are concerned.

A. F. T.

APPENDIX

LIST OF EQUIPMENT

Saddle, bit and bridle
Saddle-bags (see sketch and description next page)
Brush for horse
Curry-comb
Pocket-knife (strong, with hoof-pick and point for making
    holes in leather)
Awl and waxed string (for mending leather ; protect point
    of awl with a cork)
Shaving tackle
Soap
Comb
Tooth brush and paste
Small towel
Scissors (in leather sheath)
Iodine (in small glass container fitting into a metal tube)
Cotton wool and gauze (small quantity, in tin)
Adhesive tape (has many uses)
Camera (small, folding)
Films or film-pack (one or two sufficient ; more can be
    bought along route)
Note-book and pencil
Maps (Ordnance Survey, $\frac{1}{2}$ inch to mile)
Pocket compass (not necessary)
2 Polo shirts
1 Change of underwear

3 large handkerchiefs
1 Pair of pyjamas (silk to facilitate washing and drying)
1 Pair of spare socks
1 Polo sweater
Raincoat (as light and thin as possible)
Travellers' cheques (carried in large leather tobacco
    pouch)
Shoes or boots and canvas leggings (never mind appearance).
    Top-boots are apt to be too hot, and, when wet,
    troublesome to take off.   Breeches not too heavy nor
    tight around the knees.

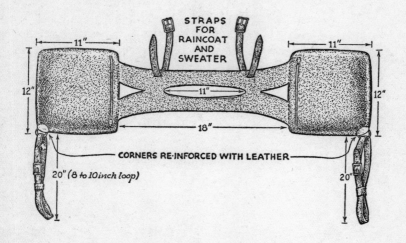

STRAPS
FOR
RAINCOAT
AND
SWEATER

11"

12"

11"

11"

12"

18"

CORNERS RE·INFORCED WITH LEATHER

20" (8 to 10 inch loop)

20"

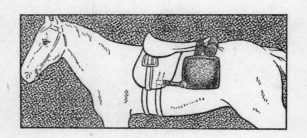